living with
GRACE

living with GRACE

Life Lessons *from* America's Princess

MARY MALLORY

Guilford, Connecticut

An imprint of The Rowman & Littlefield Publishing Group, Inc.
4501 Forbes Blvd., Ste. 200
Lanham, MD 20706
www.rowman.com

Distributed by NATIONAL BOOK NETWORK

British Library Cataloguing in Publication Information available

Library of Congress Cataloging-in-Publication Data available

ISBN 978-1-4930-3050-7 (hardcover)
ISBN 978-1-4930-3687-5 (e-book)

♾™ The paper used in this publication meets the minimum requirements of American National Standard for Information Sciences—Permanence of Paper for Printed Library Materials, ANSI/NISO Z39.48-1992.

Printed in the United States of America

Contents

Reviewing costume designs on the set of *To Catch a Thief*, 1955

Introduction

Poised, cultured, elegant, and unforgettable, Grace Kelly had the aura of a princess, a storybook vision come to life. She embodied her name. To live with grace is to bring polish, flair, and serenity to each day. In her all-too-short life, she realized the dreams of many, becoming a fashion icon, an actress, and a humanitarian. Her innate sense of style popularized the casual, all-American look of the 1950s. Her acting left a legacy of work that still speaks to audiences. Her determination to make the world a better place informed her later life.

"I think of myself as a modern, contemporary woman who has had to deal with all kinds of problems that many women today have had to deal with." —Grace

Born and raised in East Falls, Pennsylvania, a suburb of Philadelphia, Grace learned ambition, decorum, and thoughtfulness from her close-knit, Irish-American family. Catholic education taught her discipline, dedication, and perseverance. She learned that anything was attainable if one was willing to work for it.

Grace ambitiously conquered the world of modeling, the new medium of television, and motion picture stardom as an award-winning actress, and as one of the world's most famous fashion plates. At a time when others sought conformity, Grace Kelly blazed her own trail. She is inspiring not as Princess, Oscar winner, or glamorous movie star, but as a smart, independent career woman who achieved enormous success pursuing her own vision.

Overcoming doubt and pressure, Grace displayed remarkable strength and foresight in chasing her dreams of fame and fortune at a time when few women aspired to work outside the home. She demanded respect and a voice in developing her career.

Grace followed her heart romantically as well, ahead of her time in pursuing passionate relationships while embodying the image of a cool snow queen. She embraced sexual fulfillment as much as she did career success.

Grace's timeless style inspired fashion design the world over at a time when hourglass figures and overt sexuality were all the rage. Her refined, graceful wardrobe and attitude offered a compelling alternative for women to copy and aspire to.

For all her success, Grace was as human, fragile, and flawed as the rest of us. Who is this woman, and what can we learn living with Grace? She balanced two dichotomies: driven career woman and gracious, tender friend, all with an air of serenity and panache.

Living with Grace offers anecdotes on how Grace achieved a successful life. If you read between the lines, you might find a small bit of divine grace to add to your own daily pursuits.

Chapter 1

LEARN YOUR
LESSONS WELL

> **❝** The Kelly
> family has been
> rich mainly in
> industriousness,
> ingenuity, and
> talent. **❞**
>
> —**MARGARET KELLY,**
>   Mother

Grace Kelly and actor Jean-Pierre Aumont, 1956

Grace Kelly and family, circa 1934

ature versus nurture. What shapes us? Is it our life experiences or our family DNA and upbringing? For Grace Kelly, everything we know about her basically evolved from growing up as a Kelly. Her parents modeled and passed on behaviors and attitudes that influenced how Grace developed her life vision and personal character. Building on her family history and choices, she found discipline and a sense of purpose that helped make her a beloved star. She sought stardom not só much to become famous as to show her family she could make it as an actress.

Kelly family life revolved around overpowering father John Brendan "Jack" Kelly Sr. The youngest of ten children born to poor Irish immigrants, Jack's gregarious personality and dynamic presence dominated his family and pushed him on to success in early twentieth-century Philadelphia. Starting adult life as a bricklayer, young Jack learned hard work and persistence and used those traits to become a millionaire in the construction business. Practicing the same principles of relentless discipline and drive also earned him three gold medals as a rower in the 1920 and 1924 Olympics. Jack parlayed this win-at-all-costs attitude into his business, making Kelly For Brickwork one of the largest and well known on the East Coast.

Achievement ran in the Kelly family, especially in the entertainment field. Jack's older brother Walter appeared in several Broadway productions, produced a recording of his stage act, and performed for years as a judge in various stage and vaudeville shows before finally acting in films. Older brother George worked in vaudeville as a writer, actor, and director before gaining fame as a renowned playwright with his satiric comedies *The Torch-Bearers* (1922), *The Show-Off* (1924), and *Craig's Wife* (1925). *Craig's Wife* earned him the Pulitzer Prize for drama in 1926. For the Kellys, life meant going above and beyond the ordinary, standing at the head of the pack. Grace learned her lessons so well she outperformed them all, achieving iconic fame as one of the world's most beautiful and talented stars.

> 66 Never be the one who takes and gives nothing in return. Everything must be earned, through work, persistence, and sincerity. 99
>
> —Jack Kelly

Jack Kelly reached for the stars in his personal life as well. He discovered his female equivalent in Margaret Katherine Majer, a daughter of German immigrants, who was successful and beautiful in her own right. A former fashion model, Majer excelled in sports as the coach and instructor for the University of Pennsylvania's Physical Education Department's women's teams. Discipline and perseverance dominated her life, as did making a good impression on others. Together she and Jack aimed to raise the perfect traditional family—well-behaved, disciplined, obedient, successful—with father Jack in control.

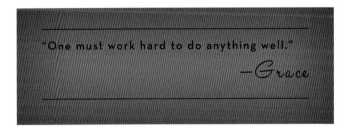

"One must work hard to do anything well."

—Grace

Four children soon followed for Jack and Margaret. Margaret (Peggy), John Jr., Grace (Gracie), and Elizabeth (Lizanne) lived a life of strict Kelly rules, with their parents telling them they could succeed at anything they put their minds to, especially sports. Life was pure competition for the aggressive Jack Kelly, improving on and achieving personal goals, while outshining others in the process. Like football coach Vince Lombardi, Jack believed, and taught his children, that life meant winning, not coming in second place.

Grace Kelly with her father, Jack

The Kelly children excelled at sports, all except Grace. Constantly sniffling, the withdrawn little girl spent most of her time alone and inside reading and making up stories. Suffering from a sway back, daddy's girl Gracie constantly found herself outshone in athletics by her more physically fit siblings. Her attempts at trying to keep up with the competitive Kelly spirit led to frustration and dismay on her father's part, relegating her to "least-likely-to-succeed status in the family."

Never one to give up, Grace practiced and strove to improve physically, eventually joining her school's field hockey team and demonstrating some athletic skills. Realizing she would never become an athletic superstar, Grace soon channeled her energies and sensitive nature into more appropriate outlets. Showing the same stick-to-it-ive-ness in solitary interests as her family did with sports, she focused her energies on subjects that dovetailed perfectly with her shy, delicate sensibilities. In later interviews, Grace revealed that "as a child I had a great imagination" and "I've always liked to make-believe." Discovering her passions for creativity and artistic pursuits, she dedicated herself to achieving greatness in them. Her persistence would eventually lead to success in almost everything she did.

> "I have to wait a long time for things I want very much. I don't always get them, but something inside won't let me give up easily."
>
> —Grace

Grace Kelly, age 2

In the Kelly family, looking good in the eyes of others trumped almost anything. Whether on top of the world or in the depths of agony, they radiated success through a display of calm and composure. While Jack demonstrated supreme self-confidence with a jaunty swagger, Margaret's firm German background emphasized keeping feelings in check. Her stoic personality and modesty rubbed off on Grace, who "never made a display of her private concerns," but instead kept them bottled up and locked away. Grace always seemed to float in on a cloud, looking like a million bucks and without a care in the world, demonstrating how first impressions often count. Without making a show of personal issues, Grace remained positive and above it all.

Opposite: Grace Kelly with her poodle

66 She had nobility—a poise and a dignity that were ageless. 99

—*THE COUNTRY GIRL*

Grace took the family dictum to heart, projecting a regal personality long before becoming Monaco's American princess. Frances Fuller, Head of the American Academy of Dramatic Arts in New York, described Grace's personality as "that extra something that means more than beauty, she practiced poise, bore inner light." Maintaining an even-keeled attitude protected Grace's feelings, making her appear relaxed and in control. This self-possession and refinement filled her with a special incandescence that just naturally put others at ease. Stanley Kramer suggested she "conveyed a natural aristocracy."

> 66 There is a mystique that surrounds Grace
> and always has from the beginning. It is
> the act she put together for survival. 99
>
> —JOHN FOREMAN, producer

Through thick and thin, the Kellys loyally stuck together, always prioritizing the family over any other relationship or opportunity. The family supported John Jr. ("Kell") in his pursuit of rowing glory, cheering him on at meets. Grace's sister Lizanne accompanied her on film shoots, often acting as chaperone. Grace often returned home to her beloved Philadelphia to visit her parents in the City of Brotherly Love

between studying in New York and making films. Shy and insecure, she sought her parents' blessings and protection in everything from roles to potential fiancées, even when

"Home is here in Philadelphia.
I never like to be away too long."

—*Grace*

Alfred Hitchcock and Grace Kelly on the set of *Dial M for Murder*, 1954

they disparaged her choices. Years later, Grace reminisced, "I was always on my mother's knee, the clinging type," seeking approval and respect. Grace displayed remarkable loyalty to her family whatever came her way, appreciative of the many opportunities they had bestowed on her even when disapproving of her choices. She gave thanks for her family's love and support.

Friendships mattered just as much to Grace. She maintained longtime relationships with friends throughout her life. From childhood classmates to modeling colleagues to movie costars, Grace stood by those who treasured her for the easygoing and

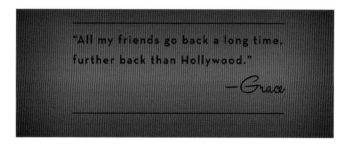

"All my friends go back a long time, further back than Hollywood."

—Grace

charming young woman hidden behind the famous exterior. She described being oneself as the best way to "win friends and take laurels in the poise and popularity field." Whenever she came home to Philadelphia, Grace visited with old chums and remained in touch through such gestures as exchanging letters, cards, gifts, and telephone calls for years. Grace's generosity and authenticity in putting others first endeared her to everyone. Her genuine concern for people was a shining example of how she nurtured and maintained long friendships.

Like father, like daughter. Just as Jack Kelly channeled his energies into becoming one of the world's greatest rowers, Grace honed her killer instinct on succeeding in acting and never let go. While she lacked the athletic genes of her parents, she inherited their strong sense of focus. Rather than sitting idly or growing distracted, Grace kept busy with the task at hand, completing it with aplomb. She and her sisters found themselves knitting if they found nothing else to do, because their mother believed that "idle hands were the devil's workshop." Instead of floundering and making mistakes, Grace's concentration allowed her to master any subject, be it learning photography or conquering acting, and succeed brilliantly. Her focus led to great achievements and accomplishments.

This fierce intensity complimented her budding imagination. When left alone while the others pursued outdoor interests, Grace spent hours making up stories about her dolls, content in her own little world. Shy and insecure as a pudgy teenager, she often withdrew into the world of books, developing her curiosity. The combination of these thoughtful traits sparked her love of acting, which bloomed into a full-fledged passion. Never waiting for good things to come her

MAKEUP DEPT.

PROD. NO. 1684 DATE 9-16-55
TITLE
NAME GRACE KELLY
CHARACTER ALEXANDRA 20.29
HDRS NO # 8
MKP NO
BASE
LIPS

> 66 There's a lot of solid jaw under that quiet
> face of hers. Grace has a single-track
> mind, and it's always in evidence. 99
>
> —EDITH HEAD, costume designer

way, Grace focused her time and energy into becoming the world's best actress. Her friend, actress Rita Gam, noted that "Grace raced through life as though it were a cavalry charge. ..." Grace provides the perfect example of how concentrating intensely on one subject can bring emotional fulfillment and untold success.

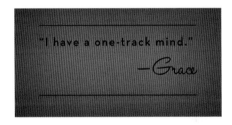

"I have a one-track mind."

—Grace

Gossip columnist Hedda Hopper captured the essence of Grace's exquisite spirit, calling her "like a dream walking." She glowed with an otherworldly charm that set her apart from mere mortals. Grace's mysterious softness and vulnerability attracted others while also engendering their protective

Opposite: *The Swan* makeup shot

feelings. Her sister Lizanne remarked, "She always had a way of getting people to do things for her. You really thought she needed help, but she did not need any help at all." Jimmy Stewart described her as "a piece of Dresden china, something slightly untouchable." Grace's delicate appearance disguised her tough-as-nails character, which she often employed to her advantage. Her special flair provided many rich opportunities for engendering relationships, offering a first-class model of how to inspire others.

---

66 Grace has always had an air of mystery about her. 99

—**FRANCES FULLER,** American Academy of Dramatic Arts chairperson

---

Part of this magical attitude stemmed from shyness, insecurity, and fears of rejection, but much of it also resulted from Grace's decision to protect her privacy. Much of her life revolved around the phrase, "Never complain, never explain." Grace seldom answered personal or probing questions from journalists and forbade Metro-Goldwyn-Mayer (MGM) to hand out her vital statistics, telling one reporter, "A person has to keep something to herself, or your life is just a layout in a magazine." One reporter later complained that obtaining a personal anecdote from Grace was "like trying to chip granite with a toothpick." While keeping secrets provided her a sense of security, it also left others curious and intrigued to know who the real Grace was. The public often asked, "Who's that girl?" Phil Santora of the *Los Angeles Daily News* described her

as an "ash-blonde enigma" in a review. Like a princess in a fairy tale, Grace projected a special mystique that left others hungry to know the real her.

---

66 Grace was glacially cool, like a wonderful sherbet in the middle of the desert. 99

—OLEG CASSINI, fashion designer

Though her family initially teased her for pursuing creative outlets rather than sports, Grace remained steadfast in her artistic endeavors, taking ballet lessons, acting classes, and performing on stage starting at the age of eleven. Grace intended to study dance at Bennington College, but entered the American Academy of Dramatic Arts in New York in 1947 after her plans fell through. Though her parents disapproved of something so frivolous, Grace moved straight ahead, determined to follow her own path. As a friend later stated about her, "Knows where she's going. Driving herself like a streamlined racing car." Once Grace made up her mind, nothing stood in her way. Her never-say-die attitude came in handy whenever she pursued new paths or chased down her dreams.

Grace quickly found work modeling for magazines and later appeared in television commercials after she made the

> "When I settled in New York . . . determined
> to become an actress, I didn't have any
> illusions as to how long it would take, and
> what I'd have to go through."
>
> —*Grace*

move to New York. She never stopped hustling in her rise to the top, aiming to conquer a field and then move on. Once becoming a successful model and commercial queen, Grace set her sights on scaling the heights of Broadway and television. Even without parental approval, Grace confidently moved ahead, following her own heart and desires. Clark Gable understood this facet of her personality, stating in an interview that " . . . in many ways she's a rugged individualist, a girl determined to lead her own life. . . . " Grace followed her own vision of happiness and success.

> 66 Grace herself is a fast worker. Her entire
> career has proceeded with the speed of
> one of the prince's favorite race cars. 99
> —MARGARET KELLY, mother

Chapter 2

FOLLOW
YOUR
DREAMS

---

66 Grace's gaze was
always focused on
wide horizons. . . . **99**

—**RITA GAM,**
actress and friend

Dial M for Murder, 1954

LOOK

15¢ JANUARY 11, 1955

GRACE KELLY
...a big year ahead

SPECIAL ISSUE

I predict for 1955

Coexistence will be the hottest issue
We'll have more prosperity
Polio will be on the way out
We'll have a cold winter, a warm spri
Yanks, Braves will meet in World Ser
...AND a dozen other forecasts

*G*race dedicated herself to creative pursuits while growing up in Philadelphia, taking ballet lessons, performing on stage, and earning rave reviews for starring in Stevens School productions. Being Jack Kelly's child, Grace understood the phrase, "Practice makes perfect." Ruth Emmert, director of the Old Academy Players' production of *Don't Feed the Animals* (1942), praised Grace's professionalism for always showing up on time and never forgetting her lines. Classmates at Stevens recognized her talents by describing her future in her senior yearbook as "a famous star of screen and radio." Grace perfected her acting skills at drama school through study and constant repetition, what *Photoplay* would later call "do-it-yourself-success." Grace never stopped learning or trying to improve on her journey to prosperity.

---

66 This is a girl who learns fast. 99

—**LOUELLA PARSONS**, gossip columnist

Opposite: *Look* magazine cover, January 11, 1955

Grace Kelly, age 12

Grace loved attending the American Academy of Dramatic Arts in New York and participating in inspiring classes such as fencing and technique in order to build a firm foundation of acting skills. Through daily exercise, she achieved regal posture and bearing and an elegant gait, all reflecting who she wanted to be. After instructors called her voice too high and twangy, a determined Grace practiced recitations, studied vocal inflection, and listened to records until she acquired a "near-British" voice with almost perfect diction, creating the "Grace Kelly accent." Her mother remarked, "We noticed that her voice was beginning to change. Instead of her old nasal whine, she was speaking in a lower, gentler register. Her sisters would make fun of her, but she would say, 'I must talk this way—for my work.'" Overlooking criticism and doubt, Grace trusted her instincts in shaping a public persona differentiating herself from fellow rivals, one that brought her enormous fame and recognition. Her willingness to take risks paid off handsomely.

German *High Noon* program

"All I want to do is act. I want to improve. I have always wanted to act."

—*Grace*

For the first time in her life, Grace rebelled against her parents' wishes when she arrived in New York City in 1947 to attend acting school. Escaping their strict and overprotective clutches, Grace could pursue her burning ambition for performing arts rather than their desires for athletic glory. Her parents' grudgingly accepted her decision to attend the American Academy of Dramatic Arts, but Jack Kelly secretly hoped "it was only a whim." Only years later after Grace took home the Oscar for her starring role in *The Country Girl* (1954) did her father recognize and understand her unique talent. Grace triumphed by succeeding on her own terms rather than chasing the dreams of her parents.

---

66 She won't take a back seat to anyone. 99

—*MODERN SCREEN magazine*

Throughout her film career, Grace turned down opportunities whenever they conflicted with her own plans. In 1950, she declined a contract with the Samuel Goldwyn Studios because it meant leaving her New York boyfriend. While under contract to MGM, Grace once again followed her own mind regarding what best suited her career, turning down roles that offered little challenge and opportunity. Grace declined starring roles in costume pictures such as *Quentin Durward* (1955) and *The Barretts of Wimpole Street* (1957), telling her friend Rita Gam, "I don't want to dress up a picture with just my face; if anyone starts using me as scenery, I'll return to New York." Once Grace mapped her route, she never deviated from it, a perfect display of independent and focused thinking.

❝ Grace had a general's sense of timing, knew when to strike and when to retreat, and always devised superb strategies. ❞

—RITA GAM, actress and friend

Growing up as part of the wealthy Kelly family, Grace attended exclusive schools such as Academy of the Assumption and Stevens School and participated in select extracurricular activities. She gained recognition in the newspaper because of her family's prominence long before achieving anything on her own. People around the Philadelphia area knew her as Jack Kelly's daughter or George Kelly's niece. While she did play on her uncle's name by using a scene from *The Torchbearers* when auditioning at drama school, Grace aimed to become famous through her own efforts, not by using family connections to get ahead. As she stated, "I knew if I started trading on the reputation of my uncles to get jobs, it was a sure way to win enemies and lose out in the theater." Grace's determination to succeed on talent rather than taking advantage of privilege left her free of any debts to benefactors and thus respected by fellow performers, proof that remaining free of obligations and earning something legitimately can be a refreshing way to get ahead.

> ❝ It was really her way of taking what she wanted from life instead of letting life take her over. ❞
>
> —RITA GAM, actress and friend

> "I was just happy because it meant that now, I, too, belonged to the family."
>
> —*Grace*

Determined Grace sought to support herself rather than living on her parents' generosity once she entered acting school. As *Modern Screen* put it, "She has always wanted to prove that she could carve out a career for herself." Surviving on her earnings would demonstrate to her parents both her resourcefulness and the strength of her ambition. Grace once remarked, "Thanks to some lucky breaks in landing choice assignments in modeling jobs, I've been able to support myself fairly well." Grace's earnings paid for living at New York's Upper East Side swanky Barbizon Hotel for Women and for purchasing a chic wardrobe. By supporting herself, Grace could live by her own rules, not those of her overbearing parents.

Grace passed her life anxious for attention and praise from parents whom she adored who failed to understand her interests. Practicing the family trait of patience, she kept waiting and hoping for a change to come their way. After winning an Academy Award in 1955, Grace prayed this would finally gain her parents' unqualified approval of her career. She never gave up dreaming that her family would one day accept her chosen profession.

"Only success counts. Anyone who doesn't have the key which opens the door is treated like a leper."

—*Grace*

After graduating from drama school, Grace threw herself into finding acting roles to further her stage career. When doors failed to open, she turned to modeling as her first stepping stone. Grace posed for magazine covers, fashion shows, and ads for such products as Old Gold cigarettes, Sanka coffee, McCall's Patterns, and Cashmere soap, earning up to $15,000 a year for her constant work. She described her time in modeling by saying, "I learned to stay on my feet until my head hurt. Every day I would leave the hotel in the morning, and I would be out until evening. If I didn't have a modeling job, I was looking for work in the theater. . . . " Grace engaged in a dedicated pursuit of her big break, seeking out enriching opportunities and appreciative of anything that came her way.

> 66 Everything just seems to unfold for Gracie. She doesn't force things; she's just patient and kind and appreciative. 99
>
> —HELEN ROSE, costume designer

Grace expanded her skills in each part she played, demonstrating her talents in ever more ambitious projects. Even while modeling, Grace sought recognition for her skills,

Opposite: Grace Kelly and William Holden at the 1955 Academy Awards

not her attractiveness. "I've always been known for my looks. I'd much rather be known for my ability." Initially landing small parts in summer stock, Grace later appeared on Broadway with renowned actor Raymond Massey in *The Father* in 1949, gaining good notices. To help pay the bills, she also acted in commercials and performed in radio plays, noting, "You take the bits along with the big parts and keep hoping. . . . " Each part refined Grace's understanding and development of character, building her confidence and impression on others. Her disciplined and thoughtful approach to shaping her career would earn her much respect.

Burning with ambition, Grace moved beyond modeling, commercials, and radio to pursue work in the new medium of television. Taking off in the early 1950s as stations exploded around the country, television required product to fill empty schedules. With laser focus, Grace searched for parts with agents and producers, socializing and introducing herself to those who could further her career. As a studio executive would later say, "Grace Kelly knows exactly what she wants and how to get it." Building connections and playing the game pushed her further down the road to success. She regularly landed roles, ones leading to better parts in top-notch productions with major talent.

Opposite: Grace Kelly stars in the 1949 Broadway production of *The Father* with Raymond Massey

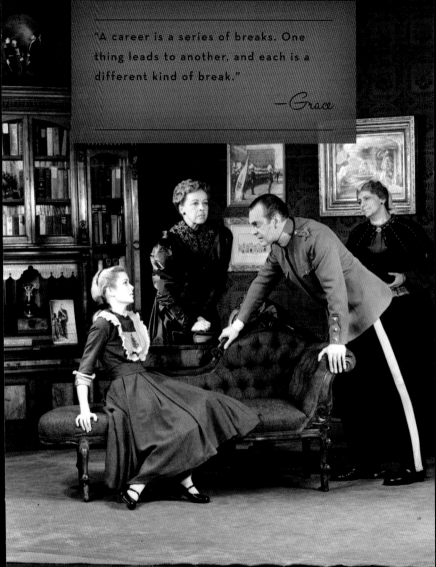

"A career is a series of breaks. One thing leads to another, and each is a different kind of break."

—Grace

"I worked in live television in the early '50s, and that was quite a challenge and very exciting. It was sort of the pioneer days of television, and it really was wonderful to be part of it."

—*Grace*

Success comes as much from acting self-confident as it does from actually possessing true talent. Insecure and uncomfortable as a child, sensitive Grace doubted everything, feeling out of place with her family and friends even though she was blessed with natural beauty, intelligence, and special talent. While landing acting roles in school shows and local stage productions drew her out of her shell, it was holding her own against talented students in her acting classes that gave Grace the perseverance to find her niche in New York. She recognized her lack of experience performing on stage and before the camera, noting, "I was terrible," but refused to wallow in self-doubt. Grace never bought into hype or negativity. Instead, she believed in herself.

Opposite: *The Swan*, 1956

"This is exactly the place I have always wanted to be!"

—*Grace*

Even after landing her first small film role in *14 Hours* (1951), Grace still felt inhibited and anxious in front of the camera. Starring in the legendary 1952 movie *High Noon* with icon Gary Cooper brought this even more into focus. Director Fred Zinnemann recalled that "She was typecast. She just had to play herself. The fact that she was really not quite ready as an actress made her that much more believable." After watching the completed film, Grace understood the accuracy of Zinnemann's criticism. She recognized every thought that played across Gary Cooper's face, while hers revealed nothing. Instead of giving up, a determined Grace worked to sharpen her technique by enrolling at Sanford Meisner's "Method" School of Acting to broaden her opportunities as an actress. Her example of developing new skills highlights the importance of growing and standing out in a constantly evolving workplace.

> ❝ Her strong determination to succeed as an actress was always tempered by inner calm and patience. ❞
>
> —**RITA GAM,** friend and actress

Opposite: *High Noon,* 1952

Chapter 3

FEED
YOUR
CURIOSITY

66 Be yourself. 99

—JAY KANTER,
Grace Kelly's agent

The Swan, 1956

Grace Kelly and Danny Kaye share coffee on the *Rear Window* set, 1954

From the time she was a child, Grace followed along to her own beat. While her family energetically charged through life, Grace remained within herself, quiet and observant. She preferred solitary pursuits to more athletic ones. Once an activity attracted her attention, however, Grace threw herself wholeheartedly into it, be it reading, swimming, or performing. Acting made her feel alive and on top of the world. Grace revealed in a fan magazine, "If you are inwardly happy, it is bound to be reflected in the way you look."

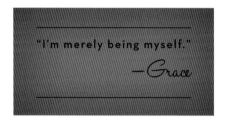

"I'm merely being myself."

—Grace

Grace enjoyed several hobbies whenever she had free time. They offered a welcome break from the stress of filmmaking, while at the same time teaching her to see the world and her craft from a new angle. Grace's love of reading spurred her curiosity, giving her insights into each character she played. Practicing piano enhanced her concentration skills while also showing how to plot direction. Shooting photographs allowed Grace to observe others and better understand human nature. Hobbies fed her imagination and supplied inspiration for her career.

"I am incapable of being bored because I remain active, enthusiastic, and curious about life."

— Grace

Live TV production on WAAM Channel 13

Grace dreamed of becoming the world's best stage actress after graduating from New York's American Academy of Dramatic Arts. She traveled across the United States to such places as Ann Arbor, Michigan; Albany, New York; and Denver, Colorado to further her ambitions, performing in summer stock productions, exploring every opportunity to develop her skills as an actress. When not traveling or working in New York, Grace often performed at the Bucks County Playhouse just outside Philadelphia to be near her family. Producer Jean Dalrymple later recalled, "Mr. Kelly loved the theater much more than he did films or television." Grace seized any chance to develop her talents and to earn the big break that would make her a star.

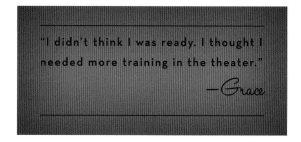

"I didn't think I was ready. I thought I needed more training in the theater."

—Grace

Just as she hunted for strong roles on stage, Grace also pursued hot parts in the new medium of television. Quick on her feet, good at memorizing and improvising, she quickly racked up a long line of credits in both commercials and television shows. Seizing any chance to expand her range, Grace appeared in serious dramas such as *A Kiss For Mr. Lincoln* (1951) and *Don Quixote* (1952) with Boris Karloff, reality shows such as *Believe It or Not* (1950), and even romantic comedies such as *The Swan* (1950, television). Television work introduced her to the grinding toil of appearing before the camera, and discovering the importance of underplaying emotion. Director Ted Post remembered that "Grace was very determined . . . " in getting ahead. Best of all, the medium exposed her work to casting directors and producers with the connections that could further her career. Grace chased new challenges and contacts on her road to success, modeling behaviors that often propel achievers to the top.

> ❝ I think that the question of whether to be or not to be an actress is one that every woman must, at some time or other in her life, decide for herself. ❞
>
> —*THE TORCH-BEARERS*, George Kelly's Play

Philco-Goodyear Television Playhouse
episode of *Ann Rutledge*, 1950

Grace intuitively recognized at a young age that building on her strengths would bring fame that much faster. Following her father's lead, she discovered the power of daily discipline and training in accomplishing goals, becoming what Raymond Massey called, "A rare kind of young person who had a hunger to learn and improve herself." Whether rehearsing or practicing, Grace aimed for improvement, advancing beyond previous successes to move forward more quickly. Combining self-knowledge and enormous drive, Grace raced toward the ultimate prize. Conquering hearts and achieving success in a variety of mediums inspired her to overcome weaknesses.

Grace once remarked, "I didn't want to be just another starlet." She discovered strengths and concentrated on employing them to her advantage, which was her way to tackle the challenging working world of which she was a part.

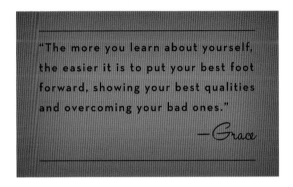

"The more you learn about yourself, the easier it is to put your best foot forward, showing your best qualities and overcoming your bad ones."

—Grace

Once on course, Grace remained forever focused on her target. Her fierce determination to succeed kept her going even during periods of doubt and despair when no one seemed to appreciate her. "In all my life, no one ever said, 'You are perfect.' People have been confused about my type, but they agreed on one thing: I was in the 'too' category—too tall, too leggy, too chinny." Proud of her looks and believing strongly in her talents, Grace never admitted defeat, seeking fame and fortune even when others grew discouraged and gave up. She shrugged off disappointment and dreamed of better days while she stalked her big break. Grace ignored naysayers and negativity in her determination to succeed, which was a perfect antidote for surviving a sometimes hostile and uncaring world.

"I'm basically a feminist. I think that women can do anything they decide to do."

—Grace

Besides discovering her strengths, Grace struggled to overcome her shortcomings. Quiet and withdrawn, she sometimes felt out of place when meeting new people, a serious deterrent to succeeding in acting. Her mother even described her as "shy and retiring." While her natural warmth attracted others, Grace never totally relaxed when around strangers. Rita Gam once remarked that "Grace doesn't talk unless she has something to say." As her self-confidence bloomed, so did her reaction to meeting new people. Grace felt more comfortable with outsiders, especially with agents or producers who could further her career. She confronted her weaknesses by repeatedly practicing new behaviors until they became natural.

> 66 She was somebody who had her act together. 99
>
> —JOHN FOREMAN, producer

Even after landing her first film role in *14 Hours*, Grace considered herself too green for movies. Inhibited and tense, she felt out of place in her small role as "lady in lawyer's office." She refused a Samuel Goldwyn Studios' long-term contract and, instead, returned to New York for stage work and in order to remain close to her boyfriend. After watching Gary Cooper steal *High Noon*, Grace remarked, it "taught me a lesson about my own inadequacies and helped me learn how to make thoughts reflect themselves in my face." Looking to feel her parts rather than play technique, Grace enrolled in "Method" acting classes to overcome her reticence in expressing emotion. She possessed the courage to confront impediments and stretch beyond her comfort zone to mature as both an actress and a person.

66 In a way, her story is an affirmation of the American dream. 99

—THEATRICAL MAIL ASSOCIATION

Grace experienced periods of enormous doubt and indecision trying to fit in and find her place. "I was terribly shy when I was young. I almost crawled into the woodwork I was so self-conscious. . . . " Participating in school plays and local productions and gaining recognition for her talents inspired Grace's self-confidence. Posing for illustrations, acting onstage, and performing on television further boosted her morale. Just acting successful encouraged Grace as well. While she gained self-assurance in managing situations, Grace remained the same down-to-earth and easygoing young lady she ever was. She demonstrated how to move through life successfully while treating others with respect.

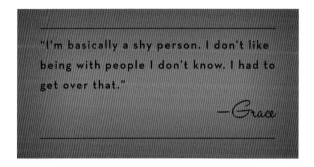

"I'm basically a shy person. I don't like being with people I don't know. I had to get over that."

—Grace

Learning how to improvise, quickly memorize lines, and go with the flow while performing on live television inspired Grace's confidence in her acting abilities. As Edith Head once explained, "She is the total professional in whatever she does." These quick thinking skills captivated film producers looking for actresses with smooth reflexes and instincts. Recognizing what roles best suited her personality gave Grace faith in choosing which parts to audition for. Being prepared when she walked on the set settled her nerves as well. The combination of all these elements prepped her to face anything that Hollywood could throw her way.

66 Grace was touching. When you played a scene with her, she really listened. Grace was right there with you. She was Buddha-like in her concentration. 99

—CARY GRANT, actor

The Country Girl, 1954

> 66 By the time she came to Hollywood she was a finished product. 99
>
> —JIMMY STEWART, actor

Thanks to Kelly family practices and her extensive acting classes and training, Grace demonstrated two behaviors sealing her reputation as the total professional: concentration and composure. Teacher Sanford Meisner's acting method forced actors to submerge technique in favor of their actual feelings at that moment, keeping them focused on the matter at hand. William Holden described Grace's impressive skill to the press. "With some actresses, you have to keep snapping them to attention like a puppy. Grace is always concentrating. In fact, she sometimes keeps me on the track." Grace always centered her attentions on the person or part on hand, remaining in the moment and thus showing her care. This habit impressed her colleagues and friends.

Maintaining her cool was a Grace Kelly trademark, leading some to call her "the ice princess." Nothing seemed to faze her. Throwing a temper tantrum or displaying attitude never crossed her mind. In fact, she would have felt mortified at causing an interruption or making such a scene. She remained

levelheaded at all times, even during tense situations. To vent her frustrations, Grace revealed, "I go away to be horrible by myself." Cary Grant described her behavior as "composure born of confidence, application, concentration, and knowledge." Grace was the consummate professional, inspiring others with her polished and unflappable attitude.

66 Grace never lost control. 99

—**RITA GAM,** actress and friend

Natalie Wood and Grace Kelly
at the Audience Awards

Chapter 4

SEEK
YOUR
PASSION

"I am going to be the
greatest film star that
Hollywood ever saw."

— Grace

To Catch a Thief, 1955

Philco-Goodyear Television Playhouse episode of *Ann Rutledge*, 1950

CHAPTER 4

After struggling for years to land additional roles on Broadway after her early success in *The Father*, Grace turned her attentions to the small screen. While she dreamed of a serious acting career, commercials and television paid the bills. The medium's growing popularity and higher exposure promised a greater chance of becoming famous and landing film roles. Working with renowned stage and screen stars inspired Grace to conquer new fields as well. "I had to go to Hollywood because I couldn't get work on Broadway." She also remarked, "I felt that I had gone as far as I could in television. There is no machinery for publicity. Audiences know your face, not your name." Feeling bored and unchallenged with television work, Grace moved on to Hollywood and the new challenges it promised. She wanted to seek out new possibilities rather than stagnate.

> The girl came to Hollywood not to expand a sweater nor to pose for pinup art but to work.
> —CARROLL RIGHTER, astrologist

Grace's first role in *14 Hours* inspired offers of studio contracts, but the throwaway part failed to leave much of an

63

impression on moviegoing audiences. Landing a costarring role opposite legend Gary Cooper in *High Noon* (1952) cemented her decision to move to Hollywood though it too, failed to gain her many accolades. Director Fred Zinnemann, however, saw how the camera loved her, acknowledging "She *looked* like a star." Grace set her sights on chasing stardom rather than stage acclaim, determined to be as serious a film actor as she was in her initial dreams of becoming Broadway's next Sarah Bernhardt. Her tenacity in pursuing film glory dazzled everyone she met, allowing her the opportunity to become a cinematic legend.

66 With the determination of a pack of Marines taking a beachhead, Grace took the leap to stardom. 99

—*PHOTOPLAY* magazine

Growing up a Kelly led the competitive Grace to aim high in whatever prize she pursued. Her perfectionist nature pushed her to perform flawlessly, by not merely completing a task, but challenging herself to soar above previous efforts. Acting in

Opposite: *Photoplay* cover, April 1956

More News! More Stories! More Pictures! ONLY 20¢

PHOTOPLAY

APRIL

GRACE KELLY

GRACE'S UNTOLD STORY

Exclusive:
MY HUSBAND DOESN'T RUN ME
AUDREY HEPBURN

Meet the Man in the Gray Flannel Suit

films was no different—she longed for demanding parts to grow as an actress. Inspired by her uncle George to take up acting, Grace also followed his advice to search out meaty roles that offered real substance, ones that would develop her skills and move her up the ladder of success. Fellow actor William Holden recognized the achievement-oriented side of her. "Grace is a woman who must keep on topping herself. It's the way she is . . . one fact I am sure: Grace will never be happy standing still." Her former acting teacher, Don Richardson, also stated, "Grace had to make a bigger splash than a pair of oars." She yearned for success, but demanded more of herself in her aims to improve, setting higher standards and goals to accomplish. Grace focused less on others' efforts and more on making hers the best they could be.

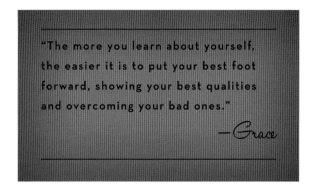

"The more you learn about yourself, the easier it is to put your best foot forward, showing your best qualities and overcoming your bad ones."

—Grace

Opposite: On the set of *The Country Girl*, 1954

> 66 At the end, she and Bing sang in *harmony* yet . . . She made a real monkey out of me because the record didn't just go Gold, it went Platinum! 99
>
> —JOHNNY GREEN, musical director

Budding star Grace sought out substantial roles that offered something new and invigorating. She received her greatest challenge in *High Society* (1956), singing onscreen with the famous crooner himself, Bing Crosby. Signing up for vocal lessons as soon as the studio offered her the part, Grace insisted she could warble the tunes herself, though the studio doubted her musical talent. Practicing with her usual dedication, she acquired a nice singing voice. Mitzi Gaynor, a fellow actress and singer, took notice, asserting, "Grace Kelly is a concentrator. That makes all the difference." Grace succeeded magnificently, laying down a simple, straight contralto and even blending in harmony with Crosby. Grace loved the challenge of acquiring and mastering a new skill, a useful trait in a career that can often throw unexpected curveballs.

Just as Grace hunted serious parts trying to earn the respect of her father, she also chased employment opportunities offering her the chance to work with seasoned professionals who could mold her talents and improve her skills. Grace originally hoped to study at Bennington College to train with renowned dancing choreographer Martha Graham and worked in *The Father* on Broadway to study at the feet of star Raymond Massey. She learned well; the *New York Times* review noted, "Grace Kelly gives a charming, pliable performance as the bewildered, brokenhearted daughter." She took roles on television with legends such as Boris Karloff and Robert Montgomery, discovering how to deal with the camera and fame. Grace searched for mentors who could provide support in bettering her technique and model a successful calling.

> ❝ Good art always looks easy. ❞
>
> —WILLIAM HOLDEN, actor

Grace practiced the same discriminating taste in seeking out motion picture work as she did in theatre and television, gravitating toward projects featuring outstanding producers and top actors. In just her second film, Grace starred opposite the great Gary Cooper in *High Noon*, with the respected Fred

“ She selects clothes and stories and directors with the same sureness. ”

—EDITH HEAD,
costume designer

Zinnemann serving as director and Stanley Kramer as producer. For her fourth movie, she worked with master director Alfred Hitchcock in *Dial M for Murder* (1954), who provided her with rich lessons. "Mr. Hitchcock taught me everything about cinema. It was thanks to him that I understood that murder scenes should be shot like love scenes and love scenes like murder scenes." Grace sought to work with the best in her field in order to expand her expertise and artistry.

Just as remarkably, Grace discerned early on what work suited her best. She channeled her energies into activities such as dancing and acting—ones demanding patience, persistence, and hard work—which permitted her to express emotions at a safe distance. Her mother remarked, "She's an emotional actress, and in spite of her cool, calm exterior, she does have feelings. In many ways, I think she is perhaps more emotional than most people." Sensitive and gentle, acting offered a safe outlet in which to release her emotions. While afraid to risk being vulnerable with many people, Grace could indirectly express passionate and conflicting feelings through her work, voicing the inner torments and emotions of the characters she portrayed. Listening to her intuition, Grace perceived the best career for employing her special talents and the one to bring her happiness.

Opposite: Alfred Hitchcock, Grace Kelly, and James Stewart
at the premiere of *Rear Window*, 1954

❝ It takes two things to make a good actor
or actress: ability and humanity. ❞

—GARY COOPER, actor

When it came to choosing parts, Grace possessed a canny instinct for picking characters similar to herself, ones who seized opportunities to flourish while demonstrating strong self-possession in achieving their goals. Each forced her to dig deep inside herself to understand life, both hers and the character's, from a new angle. The ones Grace chose, such as the part of Lisa Fremont in *Rear Window* (1954), allowed her luminous personality to shine through, the one that audiences fell in love with, while at the same time teaching her something new about herself. She possessed what Alfred Hitchcock called " . . . a presence . . . a charisma," an incandescence that just jumped off the screen. Grace played up her best assets and impressed others by embodying her authentic self onscreen.

❝ Grace Kelly had both natural beauty and
an indefinable quality of attractiveness
that were apparent to everyone. ❞

—ANDY ROONEY, newspaper columnist

At the beginning of her television and film career, Grace excelled by practicing dramatic techniques learned through her study at the American Academy of Dramatic Arts. She worked from the outside in, realistically capturing the movements and mannerisms of her characters, all while remaining restrained in revealing emotion. Recognizing a need to unlock her expressive potential, she dedicated a year to studying acting in guru Sanford Meisner's Neighborhood Playhouse, acting that combined instinct with imagination. Meisner preached, "Repetition leads to impulse. You have to learn how not to think any more, and how to act before you think." Practicing this technique permitted Grace to trust her feelings and reveal her vulnerabilities onscreen as well as to better read people and situations in real life.

> 66 You start discovering her the day you meet her, and you go right on discovering her as the picture progresses. 99
>
> —GEORGE SEATON, director

Learning these new techniques deepened Grace's acting, making her performances leap off the screen. Letting go of her own emotional reticence, she brought her deep, buried feelings to the surface. Unforced and natural, her characters grew richer and more expressive, full of emotion. Grace openly shared scenes with other performers rather than acting at them. Many of her fellow actors described how they felt completely at ease with her, running a scene as if it were a conversation in real life. Frequent costar William Holden revealed, "She has the courage to be vulnerable." Letting down her guard freed Grace's acting and potential.

> 66 Grace doesn't throw everything at you in the first five seconds. Some girls give you everything they've got at once and there it is—there is no more. But Grace is like a kaleidoscope—one twist and you get a whole new facet. 99
>
> —GEORGE SEATON, director

In many ways, acting forced Grace to step outside her comfort zone and go with the flow. Shy and introverted, she preferred intimate groups to large, noisy crowds. On film sets, however, a crew consisted of a small army of people working together to complete each movie production. The hectic and disorganized world of filmmaking conflicted with Grace's orderly and calm approach to life. Participating in making a

On the set of *High Noon*, 1952

The Bridges at Toko-Ri, 1954

movie forced her to let go of control and practice all the powers of concentration gained from studying "The Method" school of acting. Grace moved beyond her fears to try something new and to trust in the process.

Along with detesting large crowds, Grace absolutely hated having to perform publicity chores. Often detached and reserved in personal situations, she resented having to open up her private life to prying journalists. Longtime friend and photographer Howell Conant revealed, "She's above the ballyhoo. She wants no part of it." While Grace found it excruciating to talk about anything with the press, she resigned herself to publicizing movies in order to get audiences to see them. She learned to play the game, though she publicly proclaimed, "Never for a moment have I sought publicity." Grace promoted projects and colleagues while keeping mum about her private life.

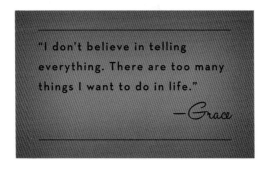

"I don't believe in telling everything. There are too many things I want to do in life."

—Grace

Photoplay Fashions

TURN
THE PAGE
FOR
DETAILS

Chapter 5

PRACTICE
GENEROSITY

---

66 She saves it all for
the camera—she's a
real pro. **99**

—HOLLYWOOD
PRODUCER

Spencer Tracy and Grace Kelly, 1954

*P*erfectionist Grace completed any task set before her with aplomb and skill, demonstrating a strong work ethic, willingness to work long hours, and to push beyond what was required in order to get things right. Her diligent preparation and attention to detail impressed others on her rise to the top. Television directors loved how she easily picked up new pieces of business and dialogue right before filming, learning to quickly improvise and think on her feet. As Grace noted, "Acting is a very time-consuming profession to do well." Grace gave 100 percent to whatever project she was working on, ensuring its success.

66 She preserves an actor's sanity. 99

—WILLIAM HOLDEN, actor

Producers loved working with Grace because of her high professional standards. She dedicated herself to making each production the best it could be, giving her total attention to the project. By the time she arrived on the set, Grace had memorized the script, practiced any necessary skills, and mastered her part. Actor William Holden acknowledged her thorough preparation to the press, declaring, "In *Toko-Ri* she was always on time, always knew her lines, and always

Opposite: *High Society*, 1956

contributed a great deal to the scene." Grace's values instilled in her the belief of always doing her best, a trait that never goes out of style.

> **❝ The most valuable property in the movies. ❞**
>
> —*LIFE* magazine

Grace seemed to "turn the world on with her smile." Her megawatt personality and dazzling grin always brightened the faces of schoolmates, family, friends, and coworkers. Grace offered a ray of sunshine that lit up movie screens as well. *The Grace Kelly Story* (1957) declared, "She is like sunlight reflected from a glacier." Photographer Bud Fraker believed that much of her appeal rested on her indescribable charm. Grace's sparkling energy truly made her a Princess Charming.

> **❝ When you look at Grace, she reminds you of a cool breeze of fresh air. ❞**
>
> —**BING CROSBY,** singer

Opposite: *High Society,* 1956

Full of compassion and concern for those around her, Grace projected no "I am a star" airs. Instead of talking about herself, she listened to what others had to say. Makeup man Wally Westmore revealed " . . . she doesn't talk much at all, but she surely is a flattering listener." Writer Erskine Johnson called her a "warmly luscious personality," one truly attentive to all going on around her. Jimmy Stewart later recalled, "I remember her so vividly . . . she had a warmth and a tenderness about her, and you could see it wasn't forced, that it wasn't her way of acting. It was the woman herself." Grace deepened her relationships and engendered kindnesses by paying real attention to those around her.

66 She not only looks terrific, she seems to be having wonderful thoughts too. 99

—HOLLYWOOD talent agent

Grace's parents recognized her remarkable serenity from an early age. Even when her younger sister Lizanne locked her in a closet, Grace remained quiet and calm for hours, happily making up stories and playing with her dolls. As Lizanne later noted, "She seemed to have been born with a serenity the rest of us didn't have." Whether dealing with overbearing, sports-obsessed parents, or stress-inducing stage and television auditions, Grace remained remarkably cool and composed, letting nothing faze her. Her stoic nature impressed friends and coworkers alike, who marveled at how even-tempered and kind she remained even during pressure-filled situations. Grace remained centered and focused on the big picture, embracing whatever challenges came her way.

66 Grace had a kind of serenity, a calmness . . . she was so relaxed in front of the camera that she made it look simple. . . . 99

—CARY GRANT, actor

Opposite: Grace Kelly and James Stewart on the set of *Rear Window*, 1954

On the set of *Dial M for Murder*, 1954

When discussing her acting, Cary Grant once remarked that Grace "had total relaxation, absolute ease—she was *totally* there." Others remarked on the graceful poise she projected. Reporter William Leonard described her as a "girl who's been a queen all her life." This innate sense of composure also functioned as a protective mask, keeping people and difficult situations at a distance. Her gentle though sometimes distant nature, which some described as cold, made her feel safe. Some Hollywood insiders remarked, "What people think is poise and dignity is just shyness." Grace's sense of ease and gentle calmness offered a pleasing antidote to the world's often loud, vulgar displays.

❝ Grace was a gentle woman, something so totally new to Hollywood. ❞

—RITA GAM, actress and friend

Growing up, Grace was never self-obsessed but full of concern toward others. Her mother introduced her and her siblings to supporting and promoting civic causes when they were young. Grace often identified with those feeling lonely or in need of help, and she remained actively involved in championing charities throughout her adult life. During her time in Hollywood, Grace visited children's hospitals, participated in Easter Seals, and promoted the City of Hope, all without seeking great publicity for her efforts. As makeup man Wally Westmore noted, "She doesn't project, as they say, around Hollywood." Grace employed her success to bring kindness to the world, all without glorifying herself, a refreshing attitude in a world so lacking of it.

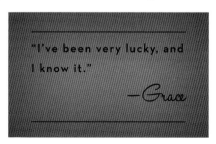

"I've been very lucky, and I know it."

—Grace

While aiming to accomplish her dreams, Grace never pushed herself ahead of others. Forever modest and humble, she promoted causes and projects rather than singing her own praises. Working to create authentic characters, Grace saw her responsibility as building on the vision of those producing each project she worked on. Unlike those seduced by fame and Hollywood glamour, Grace remained levelheaded and realistic, always looking to be part of the creative process and not the prima donna above it. A friend could truthfully tell *Time* magazine in 1953, "Here, for the first time in history, is a babe that Hollywood can't get to." Grace never forgot where she came from and refused to play games. She remained humble and easygoing, and her authenticity inspired legions of fans.

> 66 We all knew from the beginning that there was something special about Grace. 99
>
> —MARGARET KELLY

Grace longed for the creative challenge and opportunities that motion pictures promised, but she sometimes grew discouraged and frustrated about both the production and publicity process. While her first starring role in *High Noon* (1952) served as a great learning opportunity, Grace felt tense

Grace Kelly at the Cannes Film Festival, 1955

and unprepared during the short production schedule. Bad material, difficult locations, and loneliness plagued *Green Fire* (1954). *Mogambo* (1953) stretched on for months in the wilds of Africa. She hated revealing personal information about herself in interviews. Grace eventually found a way to triumph over adversity, declaring, "I've never been depressed by my work. If it became a chore, I'd give it up." She buttoned up complaints, found the best of any situation, and remained grateful for opportunities, overcoming her sense of frustration and disappointment.

"I loved acting. I loved working in the theatre and pictures. I didn't particularly like being a movie star. There's a big difference."

—*Grace*

On the other hand, Grace adored participating in projects that offered roles of substance and opportunities to advance her craft. She enjoyed her time with Alfred Hitchcock, feeling an inspired connection with the British director. Her blonde beauty fit in perfectly with his vision of a "snow princess," virginal on the exterior but a passionate volcano underneath. Their talents meshed in creating sensual, self-assured female characters. *The Country Girl* (1954) fully revealed her acting prowess, forcing her to dig deep within herself for dark, bitter, and hard emotions. *High Society* (1956) brought her together with old friends in a frothy, entertaining musical. As with most of her life, Grace could truthfully say, "I've just had fantastic luck I guess." While she did experience great luck, Grace also remained choosy in selecting projects, displaying a sure hand in picking films and coworkers. Grace's discriminating taste helped her build a career rather than just fall into anything that came her way.

66 She'll be different in every movie she makes. Not only because of makeup or clothes but because she plays a character from the inside out. There's no one else like her in Hollywood. 99

—**ALFRED HITCHCOCK,** director

Along the way, Grace received excellent supervision and guidance from a variety of helpful people. Her uncle George inspired and encouraged her to take up acting, suggesting she hold out for more serious roles, while cautioning about the nature of stars' indentured servitude to Hollywood studios. Director Alfred Hitchcock motivated Grace to finally surrender her self-consciousness and truly inhabit her roles. His attraction and devotion paid dividends, bringing out the sensuality hidden beneath her innocent facade. As he described it, "An actress like her gives the director certain advantages." Grace remained open to direction from those more experienced than she.

> 66 In Miss Kelly, the American screen seems to have found an actress with all the potential of another Garbo. 99
>
> —*THE HOLLYWOOD REPORTER* review

At the same time, Grace offered career assistance by providing suggestions and information to others looking to break into show business. Her early television success inspired many of her acting school friends and acquaintances to seek her wisdom on trying to succeed in the field. She laughingly revealed years later trying to discourage an inexperienced young actor named Paul Newman by saying, "I tried to find a kind way of letting him know that he wasn't going to make it." She did provide integral help in promoting others just beginning their careers. After a rising young photographer named Howell Conant shot striking, sensuous photos of her for a magazine layout, Grace began requesting him for more and more sessions, making his career. She practiced the same generosity shown her by assisting others in their rise to success.

> 66 Almost everything happened after I became famous with Grace. 99
>
> —HOWELL CONANT, photographer

Mogambo, 1953

Best Wishes Grace Kelly

Chapter 6

TAKE
RISKS

> **❝** I saw she was
> a woman of
> confidence,
> and not just
> a little girl. **❞**
>
> —SAM ZIMBALIST,
> producer

The Swan, 1956

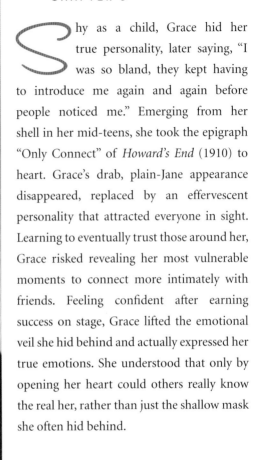

Shy as a child, Grace hid her true personality, later saying, "I was so bland, they kept having to introduce me again and again before people noticed me." Emerging from her shell in her mid-teens, she took the epigraph "Only Connect" of *Howard's End* (1910) to heart. Grace's drab, plain-Jane appearance disappeared, replaced by an effervescent personality that attracted everyone in sight. Learning to eventually trust those around her, Grace risked revealing her most vulnerable moments to connect more intimately with friends. Feeling confident after earning success on stage, Grace lifted the emotional veil she hid behind and actually expressed her true emotions. She understood that only by opening her heart could others really know the real her, rather than just the shallow mask she often hid behind.

The Country Girl, 1954

> 66 Grace is extremely vulnerable in being entirely herself, both off-screen and on. 99
>
> —WILLIAM HOLDEN, actor

Once she blossomed into an angelic looking teenager, Grace's attraction to boys took off, as did their attentions toward her. With that delicate, china doll look of hers, males fell all over themselves in their attempts to get next to her. Producer Joshua Logan once revealed, "Grace could seduce a man with just a look from those big warm eyes," wrapping them around her little finger. While all the attention flattered her, Grace sometimes employed it to her advantage. Pretending to be in love onscreen with some of the most attractive men on the planet also brought out both her tenderness and her tendency to fall in love easily. Romance highlighted Grace's softness and vulnerability, giving her the confidence to let down her guard, express her feelings, and reveal her tender side.

Opposite: *Rear Window*, 1954

> ❝ She must have struck men the same way she struck me. Every man who knew her from the time she was about fifteen and even before that wanted to take care of Gracie. ❞
>
> —MARGARET KELLY

As early as high school, guys young and old fell at the feet of the gorgeous Grace. Her sisters joked, "She had a million boyfriends." Thanks to her dazzling good looks, playfulness, and delicate mystique, men found Grace irresistible. Putting on her best smiles and come-hither looks, Grace had her pick of young hunks from Philadelphia to New York, trying out what she liked and didn't like in her search for Mr. Right. Grace enjoyed many a night out on the town, with her sweet appearance disguising a wild, passionate side that she freely let rip. Later joking about a one-time experience in a high school boyfriend's old car, she laughed, "I hope it's safely in the scrapyard. Just think of the tales that backseat could tell!" Though affectionate and playful, Grace practiced discretion in her romantic relationships.

Opposite: NBC TV portrait, circa 1951

66 She had sex beneath that cool exterior. 99

—SAM ZIMBALIST, producer

While she chased her dreams of acting success, Grace continued her hunt for "the one." Her busy schedule prevented much of anything serious happening, but she continued adding to her list of traits desired in her significant other. As *Modern Screen* wrote, "Grace Kelly likes men and men like Kelly." Grace remained open to dating a wide variety of guys, going out with single and divorced, religious and nonreligious, young and even middle-aged men, as long as she felt some kind of spark. As she herself knew, "Most things attractive in a person are things you cannot describe." Unlike most women of her day, Grace threw caution to the wind, and sometimes pursued men for whom she felt attraction, fulfilling her own sexual needs. In other words, she didn't sit at home waiting for the phone to ring. Grace offered a refreshing example of courage and liberation in dating.

Publicity shot for *To Catch a Thief*, 1955

> 66 I'm old enough to be the girl's father, but if I were fifteen years younger, I'd be standing in line with the rest of her beaux. 99
>
> —CLARK GABLE, actor

Thanks to all of her reading and playful imagination, Grace fell in love easily with most of the men she dated in search of the white knight to give her a "happily ever after." She confessed to her friend Judy Kanter, "I have been falling in love since I was fourteen, and my parents have never approved of anyone I was in love with." Many beaux fell for her quickly too, as a *Hollywood Reporter* reviewer noted, "She makes you feel you are in love as you watch her." Sensual and playful, she easily gave her heart to her boyfriends, replacing the love she failed to receive from her father with romantic relationships that made her happy. While her father enjoyed seeing a crowd of young men buzzing around his daughter, no one ever seemed to match his vision of the perfect partner for her. During her search for Mr. Right, Grace bought into romantic fairy tales just like many of the women of her generation, without marrying the first one who came along. She merely hunted for her complementary partner and best friend, the kind that tends to stick around.

> **❝** Her premiere talent, you might say, is that
> she inspires great passion. **❞**
>
> —FILM producer

Many of Grace's hunky male costars also swooned over her charming good looks. Handsome William Holden whistled, "Now that's what I call sex appeal—with class!" Taking her movie roles to heart, Grace herself often fell desperately in love with these attractive admirers, many of them unavailable. Her friend Rita Gam remembered, "She kept falling in love with all the wrong men." At one time or another, Grace was linked with Holden, Gary Cooper, Clark Gable, Jean-Pierre Aumont, Ray Milland, Oleg Cassini, and Bing Crosby, some of whom were married and many older than she, raising eyebrows in Hollywood and various fan magazines. Grace never gave up searching for Mr. Right, surviving rebounds, players, married men, and bad boys on her journey.

While happy with her enormous screen success, Grace dreamed of finding her true love, raising a family, and making a home. She hunted for a partner who shared her values, possessed a strong, commanding personality, and enjoyed his

Opposite: *Green Fire*, 1954

"The kind of girl who may not have inner fires smoldering through her eyes but whom you nevertheless feel has a pilot light hung in case the right guy comes along."

—*HOLLYWOOD CITIZEN NEWS* review

own list of brilliant accomplishments. During the production of *Mogambo* (1953), Grace fell in love with the dashing "King of Hollywood" Clark Gable, twenty-eight years her elder. Costar Ava Gardner, recognized the signs. "Gracie was a good Catholic girl, and she was having a hard time feeling the way she did about Clark." Between takes, Grace and Clark spent virtually all their free time together, driving around the bush, swimming, and taking trips around the country. While Clark met many of her requirements, he wasn't looking to settle down. Grace searched for that special person to both match her sensibilities and desire to get married and start a family.

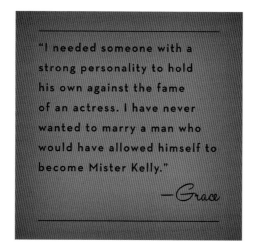

"I needed someone with a strong personality to hold his own against the fame of an actress. I have never wanted to marry a man who would have allowed himself to become Mister Kelly."

—*Grace*

As devoted to searching for Mr. Right as she was to becoming one of Hollywood's top movie actresses, Grace enjoyed her time with the opposite sex and often made the first move. She could play the perfect partner as well as the swinging playmate, but her sentiments echoed that of the Tracy Lord character in *High Society* (1956), " . . . I don't want to be worshipped, I want to be loved." While debonair William Holden possessed a wicked sense of humor and searching intelligence, he remained a married man. Practicing Catholic and widower Bing Crosby fulfilled many of her qualifications, but he looked and acted too old. Urbane French actor and war hero Jean-Pierre Aumont shared a love of the theatre and arts, but lacked the necessary passion to knock her off her feet. Sophisticated fashion designer Oleg Cassini loved to travel and enjoyed the finer things of life, but he was a two-time divorcee. Sensitive Grace hunted for a partner who both adored and understood the real her, not the one who graced magazine covers, and she remained on the hunt for true love.

66 In all her roles she is a partner to a man, not a playmate . . . 99

—*THE GRACE KELLY STORY*

Once too insecure and frightened to come out of the shadows or speak her own mind, Grace's time on stage gave her courage and voice. The timid girl afraid of almost everything shocked her parents when she asked about auditioning to attend the American Academy of Dramatic Arts, discovering the power of honesty. It became one of Grace's signature elements " . . . the Grace Kelly Look—a deep honesty that men respect and women aspire to." When offered a long-term contract with MGM Studios after the success of *High Noon* (1952), Grace seriously considered turning it down, not looking to serve seven years of indentured servitude. Instead, she requested certain conditions to sign on the dotted line: the freedom to appear in stage plays, the right to continue living in New York, and a limited schedule of three films per year. Grace learned to speak up and demand her own rights, realizing she would never achieve anything without asking for it. Her example lives on in the many women who fight for the right to be heard.

❝ She's like a hawk circling over its prey. When she sees a role she wants, she zooms in and grabs it. ❞

—HOLLYWOOD actor

Opposite: A Spanish-language ad for *Dial M for Murder*

> "If I can't play the roles I want, there is no point in my being in this business. I'll pack up and go home."
>
> —*Grace*

Grace possessed an uncanny knack for choosing the right parts and films to further her career. Rather than waiting for MGM to find her suitable roles, she shopped for good stories and characters on which to build her acting resume. While awaiting MGM projects, she worked with Alfred Hitchcock on *Dial M for Murder* (1954) at Warner Bros. and *Rear Window* (1954) at Paramount. Grace later turned down many of the parts MGM offered her: the costume picture *Quentin Durward* (1955), the film noir *The Cobweb* (1955), and the western *Tribute to a Bad Man* (1956). She revealed to a journalist why she turned down *Quentin Durward*: "All I'd do would be to wear thirty-five different costumes, and look pretty and frightened." After reading the powerful *The Country Girl* (1954) script and realizing the dramatic potential of playing Georgie Elgin, Grace confronted MGM production chief Dore Schary, insisting she be loaned out to play the role. Grace refused to sit around and wait for good scripts to come her way, taking charge of discovering good material to build her career.

Grace specifically signed a long-term contract with MGM for the purpose of traveling to Africa for the filming of *Mogambo*. She stated, "*Mogambo* had three things that interested me: John Ford, Clark Gable, and a trip to Africa with expenses paid. If *Mogambo* had been made in Arizona, I wouldn't have done it." When not filming, Grace toured the countryside, delighting in seeing the people, the gorgeous landscape, and its exotic animals. When costar Gable inquired why she accompanied him on hunting trips, she replied, "Because I want to be able to tell my children, even my grandchildren, that I went on safaris in Africa." Grace recognized that there was more to life than what was happening just right outside her window, and she dreamed of discovering it. Her curiosity and inquisitiveness continually broadened her horizons.

"I wouldn't have missed this for anything. I love to work on locations because I get to learn something everywhere I go."

— *Grace*

Grace treasured the joy of exploring unknown lands and her own interior landscape. She often traveled on assignments during her career, choosing jobs requiring location shooting in exotic regions. While disappointed with the uninspiring script, she agreed to star in *Green Fire* (1954) just for the opportunity of working in Colombia and South America. Though she later called the film "a wretched experience" because of the heat, dust, and depressing conditions, Grace enjoyed traveling the gorgeous countryside. Upon completing *Green Fire*, Grace excitedly flew to France for the thrilling prospect of filming *To Catch a Thief* (1955) in Cannes with her mentor Alfred Hitchcock and the suave Cary Grant. During breaks in filming, she enjoyed romantic picnics and strolling along the sunny beach with new beau, Oleg Cassini. Grace examined what it meant to be a citizen of the world and not just of her own hometown, observing life from different angles.

"I've seen Europe from three viewpoints: that of the tourist, the working model, and the working actress."

—Grace

To Catch a Thief, 1955

Chapter 7

TAKE THE
HIGH ROAD

> 66 She is a novelty,
> an actress who is a
> lady without being
> starchy. 99
>
> —SIDNEY SKOLSKY,
> journalist

Grace Kelly with agent Jay Kanter at the Stork Club, 1954

*J*ack and Margaret Kelly raised their children to believe in following through on promises and commitments. Grace took this philosophy to heart, putting her convictions into operation. As her friend and former agent Jay Kanter described her, "Grace was very honorable. She would not promise something and not do it." Though she often stated, "I never believed in the studio system," Grace lived up to the terms of her detestable MGM contract. While she took challenging parts in films produced at other studios, Grace remained unfulfilled by the work MGM offered her. She followed all terms of her contract precisely though, consulting with the studio about parts and scripts even though they tested her patience with throwaway roles in forgettable films such as *Green Fire* (1954). By taking the high road, Grace demonstrated her integrity time and time again.

> 66 I'd say she is one of the finest young actresses on the American stage or screen today, but more important, she is the type of girl who will always be a credit to her family and her background. 99
>
> —JOHN FORD, director

> ❝ She did everything by example, to make it important for others. ❞
>
> —RITA GAM, actress and friend

Grace followed this same strict moral code in her relationships with others. She always practiced the "golden rule," treating others with the same respect and kindness she believed she deserved. She recognized no favorites on movie sets, behaving with the same dignity and class whether talking to kings or support staff. Actor John Erickson, who appeared with her in *Green Fire,* called Grace "the least prima-donna-like actress I ever knew." A wardrobe woman on one of her films revealed in an interview: "She's so nice she doesn't seem like other actresses. By that, I mean that she's undemanding . . . she never asks anyone to do anything she can do for herself." Near the end of her life, Grace remarked, "I'd like to be remembered as a decent human being . . . and a caring one." Grace's unassuming and humble nature inspired everyone she came in contact with, and is part of what makes her such a legendary figure.

Opposite: *Green Fire,* 1954

Grace's naturally upbeat manner charmed those she met. Never gloomy or critical, her positive and easygoing attitude radiated self-confidence. She practiced keeping up appearances during tough times, smiling her way through difficult situations, and never cutting someone else down in public. Grace sometimes found this difficult after experiencing some of Hollywood's backhanded compliments. "Hollywood amuses me. Holier-than-thou for the public and unholier-than-the-devil in reality . . . I hated Hollywood. It's a town without pity." The consummate pleaser in her worked to keep everyone happy while ignoring distasteful situations.

The Country Girl, 1954

66 Grace has always minded her own
business and kept her own counsel. 99

—**SIR ALEC GUINNESS**, actor

As fast as Grace zoomed to the pinnacle of Hollywood celebrity, so did gossip about her romantic relationships with some of her famous male costars. Her sometimes risky behavior with men often led to strongly hinted accusations about her "fast" reputation in fan magazines and newspapers. Understanding the jeopardy such gossip posed to her career image, Grace just smiled and moved on, though it angered her. "As an unmarried woman, I was thought to be a danger. Other women looked at me as a rival, and it pained me a great deal. . . . " Grace truly fell in love with her costars, thanks to mutual attraction and her ardently romantic nature. Biting her tongue and minding her own business allowed resentment and gossip to just melt away. Grace displayed decency, respect, and refinement to every person she met, regardless of the relationship.

66 There was bound to be a lot of gossip about Grace because she committed the unforgivable sin in Hollywood—she minded her own business. But for that very reason, the talk couldn't touch her. 99

—PAUL DOUGLAS, actor

Opposite: Grace Kelly and Oleg Cassini, 1954

Praising others for helping her quest for stardom remained a big part of Grace's life. She owed a large share of her fame and fortune to many mentors who provided training and assistance along the way. After winning the Oscar for Best Actress for her role in the 1954 film *The Country Girl* at the 1955 Academy Awards ceremony, Grace thoughtfully telephoned Don Richardson, her former teacher and boyfriend. She expressed gratitude for his early confidence in her by stating, "Thank you, darling." When commercial photographer Howell Conant shot a fabulous series of photos showing Grace at her sensual best for a 1954 issue of *Collier's* magazine, she reciprocated by employing him almost exclusively as her personal photographer for the rest of her life. Remaining gracious and thankful demonstrated just a tiny bit of Grace's gentle, unassuming personality, revealing how she towered over so many in her generation and beyond.

> ❝ Grace has class in all capital letters. ❞
>
> —FILM producer

Grace always thanked her lucky stars for snagging the role of Georgie Elgin in *The Country Girl*, all due to her impressing its producers, William Perlberg and George Seaton, with her talent and attitude on their film *The Bridges of Toko-Ri* (1954). At first considering her too beautiful for the part, they quickly discovered her remarkable acting ability and hired her to play the role. From the beginning, Perlberg had realized, "The girl who wins this part wins the Oscar." Downplaying her natural good looks and emphasizing the bitter, angry woman's transformation, Grace won the Academy Award for Best Actress for her role in the film. Surprised and overwhelmed by the honor, she could only stammer, "The thrill of this moment keeps me from saying how I really feel. I can only say thank you with all my heart to all who made this possible for me." Grace's classy response displayed her lack of pretension and ego, revealing her thoughtful appreciation for those who helped her along the way.

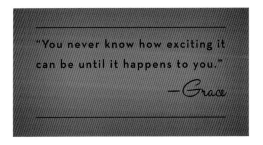

"You never know how exciting it can be until it happens to you."

—Grace

The *Oxford English Dictionary* defines grace as "smoothness and elegance of movement," a definition that suits Grace to a T. She appeared to float through life like a swan, never seeming to break a sweat or set a foot wrong. The entrance of Grace's character Lisa Fremont in *Rear Window* (1954) demonstrates Grace's poise perfectly, one of the most breathtaking romantic images put on film. She glides in to one of the largest close-ups ever as she kisses her boyfriend Jeff gently on the mouth, a vision of otherworldly elegance. Remaining totally in the moment allowed Grace to stay calm and relaxed.

Grace Kelly presented with a medal from the Treasury Department for her contribution to the US Savings Bond Program, 1956

66 Grace was born to be a princess. 99

—JEAN-PIERRE AUMONT, actor

Always keeping her cool, Grace exuded a special poise that offered ladylike charm as a cover for roiling emotions beneath. She appeared to be "Too talented, too beautiful, too sophisticated, too perfect," just as Jimmy Stewart's character L. B. Jeffries in *Rear Window* described her character Lisa, a romantic vision come to life. In reality, Grace felt pressure on all sides, from trying to gain her father's approval or living up to studio expectations. Never forcing situations, she took life as it came, rolling with the punches in order to decrease any drama. Fashion designer Oleg Cassini fell in love with her at first sight in 1953, turning on the charm, ardently pursuing her. Grace slowed things down, allowing the relationship to build smoothly and gradually. When she departed for France to film *To Catch a Thief* in 1954, Grace swiftly raised the stakes, sending him a note reading, "Those who love me, follow me." A passionate relationship soon exploded. Grace never forced circumstances and instead allowed events to happen naturally.

66 Clean cut, ladylike, cool, and serene person of quiet elegance. 99

—*THE CHICAGO TRIBUNE* magazine

Grace truly loved people, displaying a genuine caring and concern for folks after she warmed up to them. It wasn't forced; it arose from her spiritual faith that the world was one big family. Many coworkers commented on her pleasing warmth throughout her career. A journalist reported that the *Mogambo* cast considered her a regular girl, normal and easy. A director called her, "As sweet and refined as sugar. . . ." A friend told *Redbook*, "She's still just a kid, bubbly and thrilled as ever over what's happening. . . ." Costar John Erickson remembered that Grace was popular among all the *Green Fire* cast and crew. Stills photographer Bud Fraker recalled, "The secret of her personality is naturalness." Grace's vivacious spirit and lively feelings just naturally drew people to her.

> 66 She was really in a class by herself as far as cooperation and friendliness are concerned. 99
>
> —JIMMY STEWART, actor

Actress Celeste Holm admired Grace's kindness and warmth toward others. "I adored her. She was thoroughly and constantly considerate of other people first." Jimmy Stewart praised her kindness as well. "She was kind to everybody, so

SCORPIO

Grace Kelly with astrologer Carroll Righter

considerate, just great, and so beautiful." Grace particularly remained attentive to children. She enjoyed growing up as part of a large family, dreaming of settling down in a happy home with her own husband and kids. Grace adored becoming an aunt to her siblings' offspring, and cherished the opportunity to spoil her friends' kids. During the making of *To Catch a Thief* in the south of France, Grace delighted in the many local urchins who flocked around her, gently touching her and posing for pictures. Grace's thoughtful and caring concern delighted those with whom she came in contact.

> "I would like to be remembered as someone who accomplished useful deeds and who was a kind and loving person. I would like to leave the memory of a human being with a correct attitude and who did her best to help others."
>
> —Grace

Practicing Catholicism provided Grace a firm foundation in surviving the stressful life of a Hollywood actor. Nurtured in the faith by her parents, she remained a devoted disciple even when living on her own, regularly attending services wherever she happened to be. They provided another dose of discipline for coping with troubled times, while helping erase whatever troubles bedeviled the week. When living in Hollywood, Grace attended Beverly Hills' Church of the Good Shepherd, known affectionately as "Our Lady of the Cadillacs." Participating in spiritual rituals kept Grace grounded, preventing fame from going to her head. She accepted life unconditionally, giving thanks, and focused on enjoying each day.

❝ She was the antithesis of the phony starlet. ❞

—OLEG CASSINI, fashion designer

Chapter 8

ENJOY
THE
MOMENT

&&No matter where
she lives, Grace
will never lose
the quality of
spontaneity. 99
—SIR ALEC GUINNESS,
actor

Grace Kelly with photographer Bud Fraker in the
Paramount portrait gallery

Romantic, adventurous Grace enjoyed once-in-a-lifetime opportunities and experiences during *Mogambo*'s (1955) African film shoot. The company shot mostly on location in the wild, roughing it by living in elaborate canvas tents for weeks at a time. When not working, Grace enjoyed spending virtually all her free time taking long walks, driving around for hours in the bush, going on safari, and taking photos of wild animals, often with her leading man Clark Gable. Each day offered a chance to experience something invigorating and out of the ordinary. Grace always remained open to spontaneity and impulse and enjoyed life to the hilt.

> ❝ This girl really knows how to operate. ❞
>
> —*PHOTOPLAY* magazine

Filming *Mogambo* in Africa gave tender Grace the opportunity to fully exploit her sentimental side. On one particular free day, Grace found a picturesque spot to read where she could also enjoy the scenery. After returning from location shooting that afternoon, Clark Gable inquired of her whereabouts and began searching for her. Finding her sitting on rocks and weeping her eyes out, he asked, "Why are you

Opposite: Grace Kelly on the set of *To Catch a Thief*, 1955

crying?" Grace sobbed, "It's the most beautiful thing in the world. I'm reading Hemingway's 'The Snows of Kilimanjaro' about the leopard in the snow, and I looked up, and I saw a lion walking along the seashore." Grace freely indulged in romantic, sentimental tendencies and fully expressed her emotions.

> 66 She was the least self-conscious actress I ever met. 99
>
> —CELESTE HOLM, actress

Grace chose film roles as much for the opportunity to learn new skills as for the prospect of gaining fame and fortune. Several of her movies required location shooting overseas, giving her the chance to learn and acquire new languages. Grace learned Spanish before going to Colombia and South America to shoot *Green Fire* (1954). She studied French before traveling to the Cote d'Azur to film *To Catch a Thief* (1955). Grace practiced speaking Swahili before flying to Africa to film *Mogambo*. British actor Donald Sinden, who played her husband in the film, recalled joining Grace and Clark Gable at a Nairobi restaurant where Grace took charge. "She ordered the entire meal for the three of us in Swahili." Grace took the opportunity to learn something new daily, a proud student in the school of life.

❝ From the moment she heard she was due to be working in Kenya, she had been swotting up on the language. ❞

—**DONALD SINDEN**, actor

Mogambo, 1953

Choosing film roles also served as a form of therapy for Grace. Digging deep into each of her parts revealed facets of her own character. She discovered new depths to her personal emotions and, at the same time, she gained explanations for some of her own actions and feelings. Grace strongly identified with the role of Alexandra in *The Swan* (1956), an aristocratic, spunky young woman who must choose whether to marry a prince after considering all of its ramifications. Her agent, Jay Kanter, remembered, "*The Swan* was one role that she was desperately anxious to do. In fact, I think it was she who suggested it." Grace contemplated her life's course of action through many of the roles she played, better understanding her own inner motivations.

Truly a woman of the world, Grace embraced everyone she came in contact with, breaking with the politics of the time. Discrimination in any form truly upset her, going against every moral and spiritual fiber of her body. During a visit to New York's famous nitery the Stork Club in 1953, Grace witnessed an act of racism that forced her to act. Famous African American performer Josephine Baker had brought friends to dinner at the exclusive club, but was denied a table and asked to leave. Outraged, Grace dashed across the restaurant to Baker, joined arms, and charged out of the restaurant, vowing never to return. She never did. Grace's stand for equality, justice, and freedom demonstrated her courage in the face of hate.

> ❝ She will probably go through life being completely misunderstood, because she usually says completely what she thinks. ❞
>
> —CARY GRANT, actor

Wherever she happened to be making a movie, Grace played the tourist, scheduling time to tour the area, visit historic and cultural sites, and examine scenic backdrops. She traveled all over Kenya during the filming of *Mogambo* exploring everything beautiful and exotic in the country. While in Colombia making *Green Fire*, Grace visited picturesque locales, taking more than 150 photos for a magazine. During the production of *The Swan*, she received an up close and personal look at the Biltmore Estate, the film's main shooting location. Grace fell in love with the South of France during the making of *To Catch a Thief*. Besides visiting religious shrines and art museums, she picnicked and visited parks with Oleg Cassini while also dining in fine restaurants with the Hitchcocks, Cary Grant, and Betsy Drake. Grace used each film shoot as a chance to educate herself about the people, beauty, and customs of every new country she visited, realizing that everything offered something to teach her.

> "I've been discovering two other artists,
> Picasso and Matisse."
>
> —*Grace*

During the making of *To Catch a Thief,* Grace sometimes looked down from the hills of southern France toward what seemed to be a secluded garden surrounded by vintage walls of stone and inquired whose it was, never dreaming it would be hers some day. "Prince Grimaldi's," screenwriter John Michael Hayes responded, noting it was located in the tiny principality of Monaco. Just a year later during the Cannes Film Festival, Grace gained the chance to visit this private oasis for a photo opportunity with the Prince himself arranged by Pierre Galante of *Paris Match.* After being kept waiting for over an hour, she received a personal tour of the gardens and private zoo from Prince Rainier, who introduced her to both his exotic animals and himself.

> "I think he's very charming."
>
> —*Grace*

April 19, 1956 Monaco postcard commemorating the Rainier-Kelly wedding

While her public persona of perfect composure suggested that Grace preferred order and control in daily living, in reality, she exhibited a strong willingness to improvise and be spontaneous. Her passion for living often exploded in unexpected ways, matching a line from *The Philadelphia Story*: "You've got fires banked down in your hearth, fires and holocausts." During the making of *Mogambo* in Africa, Grace enjoyed going for an unusual spur-of-the-moment swim with outdoorsman Clark Gable. She wrote her secretary Prudence Wise describing how the couple stripped down to their underwear for an exhilarating "skinny-dip" in Lake Victoria.

Calender cover featuring Grace Kelly

Grace often happily stepped outside her comfort zone to relish once-in-a-lifetime opportunities.

66 She's a great sport. 99

—CLARK GABLE, actor

The twenty-three-year-old Grace truly let her hair down during the filming of *Mogambo*. Besides spending time with the much older Gable, she befriended the carefree and wild Ava Gardner. In the evenings after shooting concluded for the day, Grace often joined Gardner and Gable in his tent for a little drinking. The virtual teetotaler tried to match her costars' consumption, but quickly discovered she lacked the stamina of the more experienced couple. Gardner noticed her friend's predicament. "Her little nose would get pink, she'd get sick, and we'd have to rescue her." Grace recognized that life is too short not to join the party, trying something unexpected at least once before concluding it wasn't her cup of tea.

> 66 Grace was mature, and prematurely
> grown-up, yet we loved in her the dizzy,
> dopey, melting, and swooning school girl
> who was never out of sight for long. 99
>
> —JUDY BALABAN QUINE, friend

Grace made every moment count in the little open time she could carve out around her movie roles. She often engaged in hobbies that provided relaxation and also deepened

Esther Williams hanging a star on Grace's dressing room door

her expressive feelings on camera. Grace loved the solitary discipline of playing piano, finding an emotional release in letting go and exploring her sensuality while also allowing her impish sense of humor to shine through when playing and singing humorous little ditties. During the filming of her last motion picture, *High Society* (1956), Grace enjoyed some free moments clowning around with Louis Armstrong as she played the piano, demonstrating that the ice princess actually could express some hot feelings. She loved hobbies that energized her mind and soul, and allowed the real Grace to magically appear.

66 She took everything so much in her stride, nothing seemed to be too much for her. 99

—JIMMY STEWART, actor

Grace took pleasure in knitting, an activity many considered old-fashioned. Taught the skill by her mother at the age of four, she practiced the craft as a way to stay busy when nothing else was going on. The steady clicking of the needles offered a relaxing respite from filming, keeping her from worrying about details. Practicing the needlecraft also gave her the opportunity to create gifts for friends and coworkers. Taking advantage of down-time while filming *Mogambo*, Grace knitted Clark Gable a pair of red wool socks for Christmas, which she pinned to his tent. She even incorporated her love of knitting into her performance of repressed, caustic Georgie Elgin in *The Country Girl* (1954). Grace loved the practice for its healthy dose of discipline, a form of meditation for her.

66 Clean cut, ladylike, cool, and serene person of quiet elegance. 99

—*CHICAGO TRIBUNE* magazine

Rear Window, 1954

Chapter 9

ACT
NATURALLY

❝ Intelligent, direct,
and unaffected. ❞

—CARY GRANT, actor

On the set of *High Noon*, 1952

G race tended to isolate herself, thanks both to her shyness and sense of privacy. Never completely comfortable with crowds, she favored the company of only a few friends rather than a large party of people. An acting school friend noted, "She was a loner. She looked like a model who came in, did her thing, and left. There were students who were in awe of her because of her beauty and that distant quality she had. . . . " While in Hollywood, Grace often stayed at home, memorizing lines, reviewing scripts, rehearsing, or just reading. What other little free time she possessed was spent going to the theatre, to museums, or even to Sunday Mass. These solitary periods also provided an opportunity both to focus on her career and to preserve her sanity. Grace enjoyed her own company, realizing she didn't need to be either the life of the party or the shy wallflower in order to win friends or get ahead.

> 66 The secret of her personality is naturalness. 99
>
> —BUD FRAKER, photographer

Though she earned high salaries as a successful model and actress, Grace remained forever frugal. During her early

Opposite: On the set of *Rear Window*, 1954

High Society, 1956

modeling days in New York when sharing cabs with friends, she always seemed to disappear right when it was time to pay the fare. Grace drove a small gold Chevrolet and shared a modest apartment with roommates Rita Gam and Prudence Wise after moving to Hollywood. Though she dressed fashionably, she bought all her clothes off the rack at department stores. Grace was displaying not only common sense by saving most of her earnings, but also demonstrating her independence and financial acumen to her skeptical father.

> 66 She'll always have the class you find in a really great race horse. 99
>
> —JIMMY STEWART, actor

Grace possessed a special radiance, an inner glow that seemed to elevate her above mere mortals. Her dazzling personality seemed to jump off the page or movie screen, taking people's breath away. That sometimes faraway look in her eyes bewitched many an admirer. Her sister Lizanne commented, "Whatever quality she had, she should have bottled it and made a fortune." The still camera loved her; her early boyfriend Don Richardson noticed how it transformed her from a pretty young woman into a striking beauty. "When you looked at that picture, you were not looking at her. You were looking at the illusion of her . . . The camera did more than love her. It was insane about her." Grace put on a brilliant smile, turned on that distinctive charm, and conquered the world.

On the set of *High Society*, 1956

66 So much of her appeal lies in her charm
and personality, that I find difficulty on
catching such elusive qualities. 99

—BUD FRAKER, photographer

Even on film, Grace sparkled with an electricity that enchanted all who saw her. Whenever she appeared in front of the camera, a hidden switch revealed an indefinable mystique that set her aglow. While Grace was a talented actress, it was this blazing hot beauty that really sold her onscreen. A propman explained the impact of her special charisma: "When you work with her, she's just another dame. But when she gets in front of those cameras, something happens. She turns it on. She goes to work. And when you see her on that screen, *wham*, she's worth it."

Edith Head costume sketch for Grace Kelly

> 66 She came across onscreen like a
> ton of dynamite. 99
>
> —JIMMY STEWART, actor

Grace met dark, sultry Rita Gam when they both worked in New York's bustling television industry, and they quickly struck up a close friendship. The two women couldn't have been more different: Grace possessed a wealthy, patrician, and Catholic background while Gam grew up in a working-class, intense, Jewish family. When they moved to West Hollywood, the two career girls lived frugally by sharing a comfy two-bedroom apartment on Sweetzer Avenue. They spent time going on double dates, and trying to learn how to cook. Gam's passionate gypsy spirit inspired Grace as she broke away from her straitlaced past and embraced her independence, while Gam treasured Grace's self-confidence, smarts, and fearlessness. Gam, who later served as one of Grace's bridesmaids, declared, "I don't think Grace changed from the minute I met her to the day she died." Grace treasured Gam for her sturdy support, motivation, and faith during life's difficult moments, the very elements that make up real friendships.

Opposite: Clarence Sinclair Bull MGM Portrait

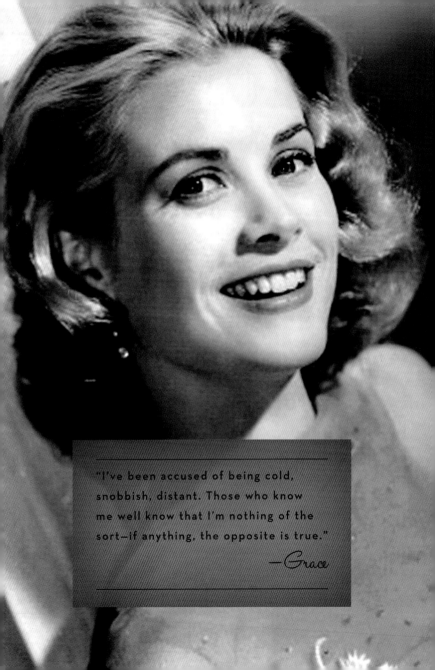

"I've been accused of being cold, snobbish, distant. Those who know me well know that I'm nothing of the sort—if anything, the opposite is true."

—Grace

Paramount fashion designer Edith Head also played a big part in Grace's life. The two women shared similar educational backgrounds, cultural interests, and love of the arts that they enthusiastically discussed over fittings and long lunches. More importantly, Head designed many of the iconic costumes that established Grace's reputation for sophisticated, stylish dressing. Edith and Grace also enjoyed a love of shopping, visiting Paris' famed Hermes boutique before production of *To Catch a Thief* (1955). Grace grew terribly excited trying on and buying gloves, dramatically going over budget with her choices. Edith pooled her money with Grace's in an attempt to cover the bill. " . . . She got the same kind of joy collecting gloves as other women did diamonds," Edith would later recall.

Grace Kelly with her sister, Peggy, and mother, Margaret, at Grace's wedding shower, 1956

66 The story illustrates that in spite of all her intelligence and business ability about contracts, in those days she still had this rather charming childish exuberance about her when it came to shopping. 99

—EDITH HEAD, costume designer

Grace's look of utter refinement masked her flirty, sensual side. Many of those close to her described her behavior as kittenish and teasing with those she cared about, very similar to her role of fashionista working girl Lisa Fremont in *Rear Window* (1954). Confident, carefree Lisa breezes in to boyfriend L. B. "Jeff" Jeffries' apartment, flashes a dazzling smile, and entices him with her spirited personality. Pulling a negligee out of her handbag, the frisky Lisa purrs "A preview of coming attractions" with a twinkle in her eye. Grace's playful flirting enticed moviegoers just as it did Hollywood's leading men.

66 People who have inner confidence are not cold. Grace has that twinkle, a touch of larceny in her eye. 99

—JIMMY STEWART, actor

Grace's character Frances Stevens in *To Catch a Thief* also closely mirrored her own independent life. An East Coast high society girl of leisure, Francie mixed Grace's combination of cool refinement and exuberant fervor. Her character gracefully makes her move on the reformed thief John Robie, played by the dashing Cary Grant, disarming him with her unexpected passion. Exuding quiet confidence in her role, Grace throws off sexy double entendres, asking him at their picnic, "Do you want a leg or a breast?," and then later in her hotel room inquires, "If you really want to see the fireworks, it's better with the lights off." Just like Francie, Grace sometimes employed a little risqué humor as a subtle form of flirtation and foreplay, two qualities that achieve more romantically than direct talk and a skimpy dress.

---

66 The basis of Miss Kelly's success is her combination of freshness, ladylike virtue, and underlying sex appeal. 99

—*LIFE* magazine

Grace always indulged her love of the creative arts, attending the ballet, opera, and theater. Her probing intelligence whetted her appetite to know more, leading her to find respected professionals to tutor her about a variety of subjects. They introduced Grace to fine arts and stylish living, sharing books, experiences, and contacts with other experts. Expanding her interest in high culture came from what actress Arlene Dahl called "results of time, training, and taste" in bettering herself and finding where she fit in. Grace never hid her intelligence or curiosity, allowing them to enrich her parts and provide a better understanding of others, refreshing attitudes that reveal her character and ambition.

> 66 She's really quite a smart little girl. 99
>
> —STEWART GRANGER, actor

She totally relaxed and let down her guard when discussing artistic pursuits with beloved friends like Edith Head. "Grace was delightful to work with because she was very well educated and we could talk about anything together—art, music, literature. She enjoyed museums. She would get excited about classical music, and she loved to converse with me about these things." Grace came fully alive talking about what she loved, demonstrating how her enthusiasm and beauty came from her authenticity.

> 66 Intelligent, sophisticated, sweet, and at
> the same time, sexy. . . . 99
>
> —*THE HOLLYWOOD REPORTER*

Never one to take things too seriously, Grace loved to joke and laugh with friends. Film colleagues recalled her kidding around and acting like a young tomboy on set. She indulged in sharing wisecracks, mimicry, and mischievous word games to stay relaxed and gleefully participated in playing practical jokes. MGM admonished *The Swan* (1956) assistant director Ridgeway Callow to treat Grace like a star, but he and the crew treated her to jokes instead. The team short-sheeted her bed while on location in North Carolina, leading her to plan practical jokes and tricks in return. After Grace heard about Sir Alec Guinness' overly devoted fan "Alice," she paid the hotel to page "Alice" in their lobby multiple times a day. The actor remarked during the making of the film, "The other day I told her a joke and Grace actually fell off the couch laughing." Grace found laughter one of the easiest ways to reduce stress and self-consciousness while also making people like her.

Green Fire, 1954

66 She really enjoyed having fun on the set; little confidences and bits of gags. 99

—**BING CROSBY,** actor

Actor Louis Jourdan recognized Grace's impish personality and sense of fun. "She had this extraordinary sense of humor, first of all, about herself, never taking herself too seriously." Grace enjoyed herself so much working on the lighthearted set of *The Swan* that she and Alec Guinness began a mischievous practical joke that continued for twenty-six years. During location shooting in North Carolina, a Native American visiting the city gifted a tomahawk to the British Guinness. Having no use for the object, the naughty actor tipped the hotel porter $1 to slip it into Grace's bed. Grace quietly returned the favor years later, somehow sneaking it between the sheets of Guinness' own

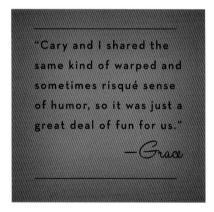

"Cary and I shared the same kind of warped and sometimes risqué sense of humor, so it was just a great deal of fun for us."

—*Grace*

bed in London. Over the next several years, the two continued pranking each other, enlisting associates to slip the tomahawk into each other's beds on opposite sides of the Atlantic. Grace enjoyed a little mischievous teasing and joking with those she cared about.

To Catch a Thief, 1955

Chapter 10

DRESS
TO
IMPRESS

> **"** Grace Kelly is an
> artist in under
> dressing. **"**
>   *—PICTUREGOER
>   MAGAZINE*

Rear Window, 1954

*G*race always aspired to the better things in life. From the time she was a child, she recognized the importance of dressing for success. Her wealthy East Falls family dressed impeccably, mimicking the style of the aristocratic blue blood Philadelphia main line crowd just out of their reach. While they might not ever be accepted as part of the elite social circle, they could look like they were. Designer Oleg Cassini described her special style to newspapers, stating that Grace "represents the new appeal, a combination of the All-American type with aristocratic bearing." Grace dressed to impress the people higher up the social and career ladder.

66 Grace Kelly broke Hollywood stereotypes, wrapping allure in a Tiffany box. 99

—KAY AND DIGBY DIEHL, writers

When she became a movie star, Grace upped her wardrobe to match her ambition of being recognized as a serious actress. Instead of emulating buxom, full-figured bombshells like Marilyn Monroe, Jane Russell, or Jayne Mansfield, she differentiated herself through classic, understated clothing. Gary Cooper acknowledged Grace's impact on Hollywood when he stated, "She's a refreshing change from all these sex girls." A *Women's Wear Daily* article described how motion pictures shaped fashion trends using Grace as a model. Liking Grace Kelly was said to be "an indication of greater maturity both in motion pictures and in public standards, an appeal that is not based on too blatant curves, too tight dresses, too lavish furs, or jewelry noteworthy only for its abundance." Grace demonstrated good taste by wearing what looked and felt right for her, thereby developing a unique style that set her apart from the crowd.

> ❝ She has a great eye and a great style. ❞
>
> —**HELEN ROSE**, costume designer

Grace never followed fads when it came to fashion, relying instead on her own innate sense of consummate style. Raised by a traditional mother who dressed her children in unadorned clothes, Grace soon turned this to her advantage. Dressing in sleek, elegant outfits focused all attention on her and complemented her graceful, gorgeous looks. Understated and tasteful, her personal wardrobe reflected a timeless sense of fashion, something that never goes out of style. As the Associated Press wrote in late 1955, "Grace Kelly, a nice girl from a nice family, has made good taste, glamorous." She

The Country Girl, 1954

realized that subtlety worked better than flamboyant, over-the-top clothes.

Much of Grace's off-camera wardrobe followed the same lines as Edith Head's no-frills but exquisite costumes designed for *Rear Window* (1954) and *To Catch a Thief* (1955). Focusing on single colors, fitted silhouettes, and long lines, the stylish, sophisticated outfits for these films emphasized Grace's delicate features and slim body type through lush and flowing fabrics. Her personal clothes also accentuated her slender frame and looks in a style easily worn by most of the female population. The *Philadelphia Sunday Bulletin* described Grace's fashion sense as graceful and soft, " . . . a matter of understatement." Edith Head explained Grace's wardrobe as, "Simple, beautifully tailored clothes giving an air of genuine elegance." Grace's superb fashion sense demonstrated that low-key could be sexy because it highlighted her natural assets and personality.

❝ I told her that her beauty should be set off like a great diamond, in very simple settings. The focus was always to be on her. ❞

—OLEG CASSINI, fashion designer

To Catch a Thief, 1955

Though she dressed simply, Grace jazzed up her wardrobe with quality accessories such as the world famous Hermes' "Kelly" bag, which she collected in multiple colors. High quality, fashionable accessories such as purses and gloves completed her ensembles, adding punch to her classic look and providing a sense of security. Grace loved gloves for a variety of reasons; they masked what she considered her too large hands, looked classy, and magnified her feminine appeal. Her sister Lizanne explained the inspiration for Grace's glove fetish. "[Our] mother was a stickler for dressing appropriately for the occasion. I am sure Mother's influence was in some way responsible for Grace's white gloves—and hats." Wearing gloves became a signature part of Grace's wardrobe, never failing to earn a mention in news stories.

> 66 Gloves and shoes are the only things where Grace loses count of money. 99
>
> —EDITH HEAD, fashion designer

Grace also adored well-made hats and shoes to complete her fashion ensembles. They added flair and superbly finished the well put together look. She always seemed to find just the right hat for any social situation, ones that complemented her outfits rather than competing for attention with them. At one of the most important occasions of her life, however, meeting Prince Rainier III for the first time at a tour of Monaco's palace gardens in 1955, Grace forgot a hat. When she appeared in her hotel lobby without wearing one, French journalist Pierre Galante explained that a lady couldn't shake hands with the Prince without wearing something to cover her head. Rushing up to her room, Grace devised an impromptu artificial flower tiara woven into her pulled-back hair, completing her fashion ensemble. She realized that looking complete suggested professionalism and success.

> 66 Stylish simplicity. 99
>
> —HELEN ROSE, fashion designer

In an interview with actress Arlene Dahl for the *Chicago Tribune* magazine in 1954, Grace revealed that working as a model helped her discover the best ways of styling her hair and organizing a wardrobe. She made the most of her assets, emphasizing her long legs, graceful neck, glowing blonde hair, and fabulous figure. Wearing solid colors highlighted her statuesque height, while open collars drew attention to her long neck. Grace's sense of style emphasized good taste and classic design, elements that helped her win the title of "Best-Dressed Woman" in 1956 from a variety of fashion outlets. The Dress Institute explained her listing by stating, "The title

"I've never thought of myself as a real beauty. I think I'm quite nice looking, but that's about it."

—*Grace*

of best-dressed woman is in no sense a synonym for wealth or extravagance in dress, but a symbol of contemporary good taste." Grace accentuated the positive by highlighting her outstanding features and special beauty, a winning concept in any fashion playbook.

Multiple fashion institutes placed Grace at the top of the Best-Dressed lists in 1955 and 1956, thanks in part to her fabulous look onscreen. The Associated Press noted, "So great has been her impact on the American public that she has started a whole new trend in the standard of film beauty and has influenced many of this year's collections." Fashion mavens praised her refined, elegant style for its soft feminine charm and youthful take on fashion, revealing how Grace was "starting to influence trends as few women have." The "Grace Kelly Look," as defined by *Women's Wear Daily,* featured a crisp, natural unpretentious, though polished, look that reflected America's can-do spirit. *Women's Wear Daily* described her philosophy as "be yourself." The magazine also revealed Grace as possessing "a fresh type of natural glamour that personifies a typically American look." This Grace Kelly Look dominated many designers' spring fashion collections, all with an emphasis on clean, uncluttered dressing. Grace did not spend a million bucks to achieve her distinctive style, but her graceful, pulled together appearance made it appear as if she did.

> "I think a pleasant appearance comes when makeup, grooming, and personality blend to reflect the inner and outer person which is the real you."
>
> —*Grace*

When not onscreen or in the public eye, Grace favored a pre-Gap wardrobe of Oxford cloth button-down shirts, jeans, Capri pants, and flats accented with scarves or belts, long before dressing casually became popular. *Women's Wear Daily* described her carefree appearance by saying, " . . . she illustrates how to be casual without flying shirttails, how to be formal without looking bizarre." Grace could be the perfect model for today's business casual look, relaxed without being sloppy. Her sartorial flair even influenced bathing suits, with designer Fred Cole in late March 1956 naming a new model "Her Serene Highness" in honor of Grace's upcoming marriage to Prince Rainier III. He announced, "Today the ideal is the ladylike look personified by Grace Kelly. And people are discovering that 'lady-like' doesn't mean sexless." Grace dressed to be taken seriously, and by looking clean, sharp, and classy, she was.

Opposite: *To Catch a Thief,* 1955

WHAT MAKES AVA RUN?

Movieland

APRIL
25 CENTS
A HILLMAN PUBLICATION

HOW HOLLYWOOD *IMPROVED*

Lana Turner
Joan Crawford
Marilyn Monroe
Rita Hayworth
Jane Powell
Liz Taylor
John Wayne
Rock Hudson
Tony Curtis
Bill Holden
Alan Ladd

———

Grace
Kelly

> 66 By wearing clothes that don't get too much notice, she gets noticed more herself. 99

—OLEG CASSINI, fashion designer

Unlike most famous fashion plates of the day, Grace achieved her stylish, easygoing appearance without breaking the bank or visiting high-end couture houses. She purchased most of her clothes off the rack at major department stores like Hudson's, Saks Fifth Avenue, and I. Magnin, or Philadelphia's own Nan Duskin, buying the highest quality outfit she could afford. Frugal Grace focused on well-made, high-end clothes guaranteed to last for years, as she seldom threw things away. Her friend Rita Gam described Grace's tight attitude toward her wardrobe by stating, "[Grace] couldn't drop something just because it went out of fashion; she was very sentimental about her clothes." At the same time, Grace showed an adept eye for mixing both high and low fashion, combining expensive suits with simple scarves and silk shirts with khaki pants. Grace focused on a few select pieces to add pizzazz to her wardrobe, demonstrating how quality and good taste never go out of style.

Opposite: *Movieland* magazine cover, April 1955

> "I just buy clothes when they take my eye, and I wear them for years."
>
> —*Grace*

Paramount fashion designer Edith Head considered good grooming one of Grace's top assets when it came to fashion. She loved how Grace knew how to stand and wear clothes, thanks to years of extensive modeling and dedicated dance practice. Head described Grace's carriage as perfect; tall and erect, showing off both her and the clothes to their best advantage. What set off Grace's understated way of dressing was her elegant posture and actual grace, or what she called, "Good grooming, cleanliness, neatness, feeling at home in what you wear." Grace appeared confident and acted like she owned the room.

> ❝ Not only does Grace have an exquisite elegance that lends itself to smart clothes, but she also has the one-time professional model's knowledge of how to wear them. ❞
>
> —EDITH HEAD, costume designer

The Swan, 1956

Grace always looked like a million bucks whenever out in public, cementing her reputation as a glamorous movie queen. Her great style didn't come from a designer wardrobe; it resulted from the professional presentation she made in always looking her best. Grace appeared meticulous and pulled together, with sparkling hair and natural makeup, and spotless, crisp clothes. Edith Head called this being fastidious about how she looked. MGM fashion designer Helen Rose described Grace's look as unaffected and clean-cut. Actress Arlene Dahl noted she followed the prerequisites of good grooming: "A healthy body, clean, shining hair, and a radiant complexion . . . " Grace demonstrated that one could be considered a fashion plate just by maintaining one's wardrobe and looking clean and orderly.

66 This look is not easy to come by, casual and unstudied though it appears. The simple, uncluttered kind of clothes she wears—and that you will be wearing this spring—demand that the wearer be groomed to the nth degree; that her hair and complexion fairly sparkle; in short be that ultimate in cool, beautiful simplicity typified by Miss K. 99

—*WOMEN'S WEAR DAILY*

Virgil Apger MGM portrait

Acknowledgments

Many people assisted with the completion of this book. Thanks to Phil Dockter for providing gorgeous images and Mike Hawks for giving invaluable help regarding identifying photographs. I am indebted to the staff of the Margaret Herrick Library who contributed most helpfully in researching this book and in finding further material. The history department of the Los Angeles Public Library, Pasadena Central Library, and Photofest also lent a helping hand. Thanks to Marc Wanamaker, Stephen Sylvester, Karie Bible, Kimberly Truhler, and especially John Bengtson for all their generosity, kindness, and advice, especially for putting up with all my questions. As always, Mark Vieira's great eye and touch helped bring both the text and photos alive. Thanks most of all to my parents for introducing me to classic films and glamorous stars such as Grace Kelly.

Thank you to Rowman & Littlefield for having confidence in me and providing me with such a wonderful opportunity to learn about both Grace Kelly and myself. Grace is a wonderful role model to emulate for her discipline, drive, ambition, and independence in pursuing goals and dreams. I admire her dignity, grace, and gentleness in daily living and for the great kindness and warmth with which she treated others. Finally, thanks to my editors Holly Rubino and Evan Helmlinger for providing enthusiasm, support, and guidance.

ARTICLES

Altoona Mirror, October 13, 1953.

American Weekly, February 21, 1954.

American Weekly, December 26, 1954.

Associated Press, October 29, 1954.

Associated Press, March 20, 1956.

Associated Press, January 8, 1956.

Associated Press, 1982.

Boston Sunday Globe, July 2, 1989.

Chicago Tribune, August 2, 1953.

Chicago Tribune, August 2, 1954.

Chicago Tribune, April 2, 1955.

Chicago Tribune, May 2, 1955.

Chicago Tribune, May 20, 1955.

Chicago Tribune, November 4, 1955.

Chicago Tribune, February 26, 1956.

Chicago Tribune, March 4, 1956.

Chicago Tribune, June 3, 1956.

Collier's, March 2, 1956.

Cosmopolitan, November 1984.

Daily Sun, August 13, 1954.

Films in Review, September 1971.

Hollywood Reporter, July 13, 1954.

Hollywood Reporter, November 29, 1954.

Hollywood Reporter, December 24, 1954.

Hollywood Citizen News, January 10, 1955.

Ladies Home Journal, March 1956.

Ladies Home Journal, October 1956.

Ladies Home Journal, May 1977.

Life, April 26, 1954.

Life, April 11, 1955.

Los Angeles Daily News, January 10, 1956.

Los Angeles Examiner, January 16, 1956.

Los Angeles Times, March 23, 1956.

Los Angeles Times, April 10, 1956.

Los Angeles Times, March 14, 1976.

Los Angeles Times, December 4, 1977.

McCall's, January 1955.

McCall's, January 1983.

Modern Screen, May 1954.

Modern Screen, July 1955.

Modern Screen, July 1956.

Movieland, August 1954.

Movieland, October 1954.

Movieland, November 1954.

Movie Stars Parade, November 1955.

New York Daily News, January 11, 1956.

New York Times, November 17, 1949.

People, August 30, 1976.

People, September 21, 1992.

People, May 8, 1995.

Philadelphia Bulletin, January 14, 1954.

Philadelphia Bulletin, November 7, 1954.

Philadelphia Bulletin, March 20, 1955.

Philadelphia Bulletin, February 26, 1956.

Philadelphia Bulletin, April 16, 1956.

Philadelphia Bulletin, July 23, 1971.

Philadelphia Inquirer, October 13, 1954.

Photoplay, April 1956.

Picturegoer, July 10, 1954.

Picturegoer, November 13, 1954.

Picturegoer, February 11, 1956.

Redbook, November 1954.

San Bernardino Sun, October 30, 1953.

San Bernardino Sun, November 13, 1954.

Screenland Plus TV-Land, December 1955.

Sydney Morning Herald, March 11, 2012.

Time, November 2, 1954.

Time, January 31, 1955.

Town and Country, May 2014.

Vanity Fair, May 2010.

Women's Wear Daily, December 1955.

Mogambo, 1953

BOOKS

Aumont, Jean-Pierre. *Sun and Shadow: An Autobiography*. New York: Norton, 1977.

Balaban Quine, Judith. *The Bridesmaids: Inside the Privileged World of Grace Kelly and Six Intimate Friends*. New York: Weidenfeld & Nicolson, 1989.

Cassini, Oleg. *In My Own Fashion: An Autobiography*. New York: Simon & Schuster, 1987.

De La Hoz, Cindy. *A Touch of Grace: How to Be a Princess, the Grace Kelly Way*. Philadelphia, PA: Running Press, 2010.

Diehl, Kay and Digby Diehl. *Remembering Grace*. New York: Time, Inc., 2007.

Eliot, Marc. *Jimmy Stewart: A Biography*. New York: Harmony, 2006.

Fishgall, Gary. *Pieces of Time: The Life of James Stewart*. New York: Scribner's, 1997.

Gam, Rita. *Actress to Actress: Memories, Profiles, Conversations*. New York: Olympic Marketing Corp., 1986.

The Grace Kelly Story. New York: Almanac Publications, 1957.

Granger, Stewart. *Sparks Fly Upward*. New York: G. P. Putnam's Sons, 1981.

Guinness, Alec. *Blessings in Disguise.* New York: Alfred A. Knopf, 1986.

Harris, Lane. *Cary Grant: A Touch of Elegance.* New York: Doubleday, 1987.

Hart-Davis, Phyllida. *Grace: The Story of a Princess.* New York: St. Martin's Press, 1982.

Haugland, Kristina. *Grace Kelly: Icon of Style to Royal Bride.* Philadelphia, Pennsylvania, Philadelphia Museum of Art, 2006.

Head, Edith and Paddy Calistro. *Edith Head's Hollywood.* New York: E. P. Dutton, Inc., 1983.

Kelly, George. *Three Plays by George Kelly: The Torch-Bearers; The Show-Off; Craig's Wife.* New York: Limelight Editions, 1999.

Kramer, Stanley. *A Mad, Mad, Mad, Mad World: A Life in Hollywood.* New York: Harcourt, 1997.

Lacey, Robert. *Grace: Her Lives–Her Loves: The Startling Royal Exposé.* New York: G. P. Putnam's Sons, 1994.

Leigh, Wendy. *True Grace: The Life and Times of an American Princess.* New York: Thomas Dunne Books, 2007.

Mitterrand, Frederic. *The Grace Kelly Years: Princess of Monaco.* Monaco: Skira Editore/Grimaldo Forum Monaco, 2007.

SOURCES

Munn, Michael. *Jimmy Stewart: The Truth Behind the Legend.* New York: Skyhorse Publishing, 2016.

Nelson, Nancy. *Evenings With Cary Grant: Recollections in His Own Words and By Those Who Knew Him Best.* New York: William Morrow & Co., 1991.

Robyns, Gwen. *Princess Grace.* New York: David McKay, 1976.

Sakol, Jeannie and Caroline Latham. *About Grace: An Intimate Notebook.* New York: Contemporary Books, 1993.

Spada, James. *Grace: Secret Lives of a Princess.* Garden City, New York: Dolphin Books, 1987.

Spoto, Donald. *High Society: The Life of Grace Kelly.* New York: Harmony Books, 2009.

Taraborelli, J. Randy. *Once Upon a Time: The Story of Princess Grace, Prince Rainier and Their Family.* New York: Warner Books, 2003.

Verlhac, Pierre-Henri and Yann-Brice Dherbier. *Grace Kelly: A Life in Pictures.* London: Pavilion Books, 2007.

Wansell, Geoffrey. *Haunted Idol: The Story of the Real Cary Grant.* New York: William Morrow & Co., 1987.

Wydra, Thilo. *Grace: A Biography.* New York: Skyhorse Publishing, 2014.

Photo Credits

Photos Courtesy of Mary Mallory:
Pages ii, v, 24, 27, 58, 65, 67, 79, 85, 99, 100, 113, 117, 121, 139, 142, 152, 155, 160, 167, 190, 193, 194, 196, 202

Photos Courtesy of Photofest:
Pages viii, xii, 2, 6, 8, 9, 11, 19, 29, 32, 35, 42, 50, 57, 78, 80, 87, 93, 95, 109, 124, 126, 131, 133 (Photographer: Bill Mark), 136, 141, 144, 147, 156, 168, 178, 186, 195

Photos Courtesy of Paramount Pictures/Photofest:
Pages vi, 55, 60, 70, 76, 88, 102, 105, 110, 123, 130, 157, 165, 175, 176, 183, 188

Photos Courtesy of Warner Bros./Photofest:
Pages 13, 22, 90

Photos Courtesy of MGM/Photofest:
Pages 16, 37, 40, 82, 98, 129, 148, 164, 173

Photos Courtesy of NBC/Photofest:
Pages 48, 62

Photos Courtesy of United Artists/Photofest
Pages 39, 75, 158

Photos Courtesy of MGM/UA/Photofest:
Page 162

Photos Courtesy of the Collections of the Margaret Herrick
Library, Academy of Motion Picture Arts and Sciences:
Pages 26, 44, 59, 106, 181

Photos Courtesy of Philip S. Dockter:
Page 153

About the Author

Mary Mallory is a motion picture archivist and historian. She is the author of *Hollywoodland, Hollywood Celebrates the Holidays, Hollywood at Play,* and *A Little Barn Started It All: The History of the Hollywood Heritage Museum* (forthcoming). She is also a blogger covering Los Angeles and motion picture history for the *LA Daily Mirror.* She lives in California.